The Pablo Helguera

MANUAL

OF CONTEMPORARY ART STYLE

The Pablo Helguera

MANUAL

OF CONTEMPORARY ART STYLE

Jorge Pinto Books Inc.
New York

The Pablo Helguera Manual of Contemporary Art Style

Originally published in Spanish with the title: *Manual de estilo del arte contemporáneo*. Tumbona Ediciones.

Book design and editorial services provided by Cox-King Multimedia (www.ckmm.com).

Cover artwork and illustration by Pablo Helguera.

The Pablo Helguera Manual of Contemporary Art Style is published under the Books in Translation series of Jorge Pinto Books Inc.

ISBN
978-0-9790766-0-2
0-9790766-0-9

For Nacho,

Who never really liked contemporary art

CONTENTS

PREFACE

The kind of work that is done in the contemporary art field is of enormous importance in our society. Those of us who work in this arena, whether as artists, curators, dealers, collectors, critics or simple dilettantes, collectively contribute to a fuller appreciation of our everyday reality in the spiritual, social and political realms. In the larger scope of history, we contribute to producing an enduring testimony and comment of the time we live in.

The art world has been in constant evolution, although some consider that, over the last century and particularly in recent years, the interest in contemporary art has waned. It has lost support, according to some, due to the general perception that the art community is exclusive, and, as others have charged, a frivolous sort of entertainment for the educated, middle and upper classes internationally. This unfortunate perception, which exists both inside and outside of the art world, was not earned but was due to a certain confusion that exists around the implicit rules that regulate this milieu.

This is why we consider it essential to finally have a *Manual of Contemporary Art Style*, such as the one we present here to you today, in order to clarify the functions of each one of the members of the art world, to erase certain behavioral taboos that exist around this world, and to openly present, once and for all, the rules that many of us follow (although implicitly, and sometimes by imitating others). You, as reader of this manual will understand (and in some cases, recognize) the subtleties of the complex (and certainly for some, strange) social and practical rituals that rule the art world. Furthermore, you will be able to perform with greater ease and success, within the professional art scene, whatever your particular role.

It is not the intention of this manual to give opinions or judgments about certain kinds of art, or to value certain art tendencies over others.

We believe that to be the job of the critic or the theoretician. Rather, this manual is designed so that the arts professional may find the right information in the appropriate strategic and social *style* (the latter referred to as *etiquette*) that must be followed in order for him to succeed in his professional activities, be it as an artist, curator, dealer, or simple aficionado, in both his public behavior and his private operations. This critical information is difficult to obtain in any other place because, despite the high sociability that characterizes the art world, very few are willing to share professional secrets pertaining to self-promotion or to commercial and creative strategy. Furthermore, the social etiquette of the art world is an art into itself, one which is until today learned only by intuition, by informal indication, or by imitation of the example set by others. Without exaggerating the relevance of the work that we present here, we consider that the publication of this manual puts an end to a century of speculations and debates around the rules of acceptable behavior in order to finally clarify them and make them accessible to all.

The reader may notice that many examples in this manual make direct reference to the New York art world. This occasional emphasis has been made in order to provide clear examples, given that it is in that city where the social dynamics are so marked and transparent. Nevertheless, the manual also provides examples and advice for those professionals that live in the isolation of peripheral communities and who still would like to perform socially at the highest level.

We would like to offer our most sincere apologies beforehand to those who may feel offended when reading this *Manual of Contemporary Art Style*. Since the manual aspires to set the basis for the best functioning and optimal evolution of the art world, it has been necessary for us to describe certain ways of behaving that many would prefer not to discuss in public. Any embarrassment caused is, unfortunately, a crucial step in meeting our fundamental objective of education. Nevertheless, we are certain that once the reader acquires the moral, ethical and professional clarity put forth in this volume, we will all benefit in the long run.

This manual has been divided into sections and includes a brief glossary that will enable the novice reader to understand certain terminology.

We sincerely hope that the reader may find this *Manual of Contemporary Art Style* a useful guide to understanding our profession. Through the process of reading this manual, we also hope the reader will acquire a richer understanding of and more cunning strategy in, his conduct in the art world of our time.

Pablo Helguera
Brooklyn/Banff, August 2005

ACKNOWLEDGEMENTS

This manual is the result of many years of gathering behind-the-scenes comments and observations by art world professionals, both from formal interviews and informal conversations. I owe the wealth of this gathered knowledge to all those with whom I have interacted over the last decade. Some informants to this project requested to remain anonymous in order to freely share their points of view. Amongst the individuals that I am happy to publicly thank are Luigi Amara and Vivian Abenshushan, who edited the Spanish version of this manual and provided greatly valuable feedback. I am also thankful to Anthony Kiendl, who generously invited me to the Banff Centre in Canada in order to finish this and other projects. I thank Ursula Davila, Irmgard Emmelhainz, David Greg Harth, Marcos Ramirez Erre, Itala Schmelz, Maria Inés Rodríguez, and Dannielle Tegeder for their many comments and suggestions. The English version of this book is possible thanks to the unflinching enthusiasm and support of Julián Zugazagoitia and Jorge Pinto. I am also grateful to Vanessa Baish, who assisted with the proofreading of the final version of this book, and to Charles King, whose editing and design expertise were of invaluable help.

Finally, during the informal distribution of some sections of this manual to art colleagues, some of them took the initiative to come up with a manual of their own, trying to publish it before. To them, who inspired me to complete the sections on imitators and forgery and who provided me with great professional motivation, I am deeply thankful.

P.H.

Men do not see things as they are,

but rather the way they wish them to be—

and are ruined.

—Machiavelli

INTRODUCTION

The Rose-Colored Glasses Syndrome

(A Realistic View of the Art World)

For those initiating their relationship with the art world, it is first important to set aside any preconception of it. One must also get rid of any sour feeling or any resentment that may have come from any prior experience in this area of work. Many of those who enter into the visual arts field—typically, the art and art history students—have a set of early experiences that has made them extremely critical of the art world. In certain cases, their disappointment is so deep that they cannot appreciate any value in art. But without being able to consider abandoning it, they remain in it, making their lives, along with the lives of those around them, even bitterer. Some of them will resort to teaching in order to sabotage the careers of the younger generation; some may choose criticism in order to sabotage the careers of all artists; and some may choose arts administration in museums in order to expand their destructive capability to include the general public. This happens, we believe, because on the onset of entrance into the art world one tends to have a bit of an idealist notion about what this world is like and expects things like spiritual or metaphysical fulfillment. One may also expect to experience a wide variety of exotic adventures and trans-cultural experiences (some of them fed with the exciting stories of, say, Gauguin in Haiti or Warhol's parties at The Factory) or the possibility of being part of a cultural elite whose profession balances intellectual sophistication with the sense of fashion. Indeed, who would not be interested in being lauded in the exclusive pages of *Artforum*, in being invited to the delirious VIP festivities in Art Basel Miami and the Venice Biennial, and in having access to free and unlimited alcohol and cocaine? What the starting art dreamer encounters, however, is a very different reality: a hostile, competitive, and highly intimidating environment. Young artists struggle to get their slides seen by curators and rejection becomes a routine experience; young curators have to work for five years in volunteer internships in small cubicles in large museums, xeroxing materials and typing checklists before they are invited into a meeting or allowed to participate in any significant decision for any exhibition. The critics rarely get paid, let alone given the opportunity to publish in the first place, and rarely do they get to decide what they want to write about. Young art historians are forced to read Rosalind Krauss' essays and have to submit to an intimidating academic hierarchy. With first experiences like this, it is natural to develop an apprehension toward the art world. But in order to overcome these first negative impressions, it is critical to understand the peculiar nature of the visual arts discipline.

Art is an uncommon profession, one that is best defined as an *entrepreneurial religion*. This is because it offers the possibility of spiritual fulfillment but at the same time it operates like any other enterprise of our capitalist world. When the novice initiates his relationship with art, he tends to see it as a spiritual calling, but secretly awaits a personal and financial remuneration that goes beyond internal fulfillment. When such remuneration is not received, it is replaced by great perplexity, distress, and bitterness. Hence, those who enter the art world emphasizing the spiritual over the pragmatic tend to become quickly disappointed, while those who go in pragmatically and with little concern for spiritual fulfillment are the ones who integrate in the field with greater ease.

Some consider it unfortunate that an activity considered transcendental and of vital relevance to the spiritual progress of humanity such as contemporary art is should be governed by economic directives, but it is necessary to accept this and to learn how to live with it, in the same way in which those who seek advancement in a religious profession have to abide by rules established by the church.

It is by learning these rules that we may finally be in the position to offer our grain of salt to the art world. If one follows the rules described in this manual and also possesses talent and dedication, one can rest assured of doing everything possible to eventually become an active and admired player in the art world.

In order to understand the complex processes which govern the art world, it is important first to clearly identify its protagonists and the many characteristics that define each one. The role played by each member of the art world is, in its own way, critical for the efficient functioning of the system. Over the years, these roles have become better defined, thus making it very easy for us to describe them here. In this manual, we will focus on the following key players, to which we have dedicated special sections in the book:

- The artist
- The curator
- The critic
- The gallerist
- The collector
- The museum director

This list does not include other important players such as the art historian, the docent, etc. We will instead emphasize the six key roles in order to better understand certain key dynamics in the art world.[1]

1 From this point forward, we will refer to the art world in this text as AW

1. THE PIECES OF THE GAME

The AW is considered by many as the most sophisticated game ever invented. In order to learn how to play it, it will be useful for the novice to imagine the AW as if it was a game of chess.

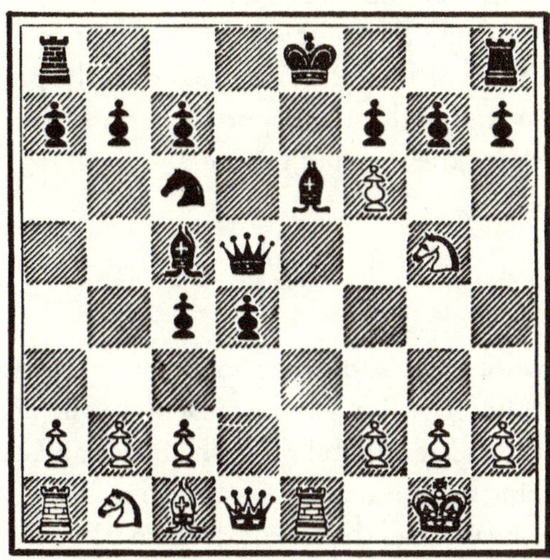

Following this premise, we find that the AW roughly contains equivalent pieces to this ancient game:

- The king (the museum director)
- The queen (the collectors and/or museum trustees)
- The curators (the rooks)
- The dealers (the knights)
- The critics (the bishops)
- The pawns (the artists).

Just as in chess, each one of these pieces moves according to the pre-established rules of the game, but in a more complex manner. The movements of the pieces, in contrast to the movement of chess pieces, can be of three kinds. There is *Social motion*, (approaching and engaging one or more players), *Financial motion* (controlling other players through art acquisition or employment), and *Political motion* (controlling the other players by placing yourself in a position of power).

We begin with the king—the museum director. This, in theory, is the key piece, because whoever captures the king either controls or wins the game. The king/museum director, however, is a piece of contradictory value. While being the most important piece in the game, he is completely powerless by himself. The king needs the protection of his institution and its staff, and, more importantly, the support of the queen (the collector and/or the museum trustees).

The queen, who, as we said, is the collector or trustee and in some countries the minister of culture, is the most powerful piece in the game. The queen has the greatest mobility on the board and can capture any other piece, making her the key piece in the game. The player's inability to maneuver her guarantees the loss of the game. It is usually the worst mistake in the game to antagonize the queen, since she is able to undo the careers of everyone else in the game, including that of the king.

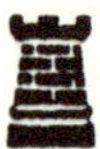

The rooks, or the curators, have unilateral powers that depend on support given by the queen and other pieces. Similarly to the way in which the power of the rooks lies in their position on the chessboard, the power of the curator varies according on his professional position in the AW. This power, generally, is transitory. On some occasions, when curators are selected to run international biennials, their selection of an artist becomes similar to the support given by the rook to a pawn during the endgame. Alliances with the rooks, as with alliances with the queen, are vital to victory in the game.

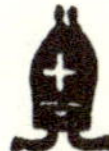

The bishops, or the critics, always move diagonally, giving the impression that they do not have any particular bias toward left or right. They are the moral weight of the game, thus their association with the religious figure. In an equally apolitical, diagonal way, the critic tends to indirectly support the artists, or the pawns, and sometimes forges links with them that are extremely difficult to break by any other piece, including the queen.

The knights or horses, or the dealers, are unpredictable pieces, usually of long reach, although with value only slightly greater than that of the pawn. They travel far and wide to international art fairs, carrying their artists with them. Well utilized, they can guarantee the success of a game. Those who mount the right horse may indeed reach success.

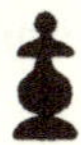

The pawns are, as we already know, the artists—the least and most important piece of the game. They are also the most populous in proportion to the total of the pieces, and given their incessant proliferation due to the art school business that produces new ones annually, it is very difficult to value them individually at the beginning of the game. Nevertheless, as they start advancing on the chessboard, they gather strength and support from other pieces around them. A pawn that advances to the top of the chessboard is considered extremely dangerous, and his or her enemies will do anything in their power to stop it. In this case, the pawn also becomes a precious piece for those who are allied with him or her. When successful, the alliance between pawn and supporter allows the pair to arrive to the eighth square to "crown," that is, to arrive at permanent recognition in art history. Once crowned, the pawn turns into a queen and is thereafter also able to maneuver with the same power as the most important piece in the game.

Game Rules

1. In the AW, there is not one single player, only two opposing players, or even two obvious colors of pieces. In art chess, the pieces have a variety of colors, determined by cultural and geographic background. On the international chessboard particularly, the rule is that there can be pieces of any color. However, the more abundant are the white pieces with a smaller percentage of pieces of other colors, as good non-white players are generally scarce. It is not desirable for non-white pieces to form alliances, unless the game is part of a regional tournament.
2. One should employ the chess term known as *Round Robin*—a tournament where everyone fights everyone. In this dynamic, all the pieces have the chance to impact their surroundings and, to a limited possibility, to win it by forming alliances according to their possibilities and powers. As always, the king and the queen are able to dictate the action more easily. When one player ascends to a higher international tournament, such as an international biennial, one will first have to face those pieces of his same origin (i.e., type and color).
3. In traditional chess, the goal is to capture the king. Although this is also true of art chess (controlling the museum director is indeed a highly desirable goal), unlike in traditional chess the primary goal of art chess is to let oneself be captured by the queen or the collector. Due to this crucial difference, art chess cannot be won exclusively by using an attack strategy, but rather by combining a technique of fighting and seduction.
4. A "tie" in art chess occurs when the pieces of the chessboard collectively block each other's movements, thus preventing anyone from winning. This condition tends to take place in certain small art communities (see the last section of "cabin fever"), and often results in uninspired exhibitions and art events.

On Rebellious Players

On certain occasions, there are those who do not wish to conform to traditional rules and attempt unorthodox strategies such as playing simultaneously as both curator and artist.

This strategy, not originally tolerated, has now become more acceptable (we will address this topic more in the "curator" section). Nevertheless, it is important to here note two details. One relates to the "single channel vision" of the AW society. Because it is extremely difficult for an individual to be remembered amidst the vast multitude of artists, curators, critics, etc., having a dual function tends to confuse people and makes it twice as hard to stay present in people's minds. Those who opt for taking hybrid occupations in the AW may not find so many problems gaining acceptance of their dual functions but rather in the side effects that may arise from such a strategy. For instance, an artist who curates must spend a quantity of time trying to change the perception that he curates only because he is not enough successful as an artist. This use of his time will distract him from both his work as an artist and as a curator. And a curator who exhibits his own artworks (especially in a show curated by him) tends to generate distrust from full-time curators who may feel that he disrespects their profession. Meanwhile artists will see the curator-artist as competition. But perhaps the least desirable hybrid combination is that of the artist and critic. In the case of writing positive reviews, the artist-critic will be regarded with suspicion and suspected of trying to forge alliances. Meanwhile writing negative reviews will generate resentment that may backfire on the career of the artist-critic. It is important to remember that there is no greater pleasure than for one artist to have the opportunity to criticize the exhibition of an artist who has himself criticized exhibitions of another artist.

2. THE PROTAGONISTS

The Museum Director

We have previously compared the museum director to the king in chess. Perhaps a more accurate comparison is the CEO of a high-risk investment corporation. The museum director specializes in spending and managing other people's money and resources, which in his case is the museum's budget and its collection. The mission of the director is to generate resources, whether they may be conservative (an endowment, or secure art historical purchases) or risky (contemporary art in general), through these transactions. While material products are necessary in order to generate revenue and security, an aggressive strategy in acquiring non-material resources, such as public or governmental response to the works of an up-and coming artist, is important to show both institutional leadership and market shrewdness. In other words, the director must attract and cater to collectors so that they may offer donations of funds or artworks to the museum. In order to do this, the museum director needs to ensure that the reputation of his institution is in a state of constant growth. Institutional reputation and financial strength go hand in hand, and a good director is defined by his ability to balance both.

Directors do not require, contrary to what may be expected, any substantial knowledge about art history. In fact, those occasional curators and/or art historians that succeed to director jobs tend to seriously damage the institution when they pursue an entirely academic or idealistic agenda with little regard for where the money is going to come from. It is far more important to have political charisma and fundraising skills.

A few rules related to interaction with directors include:

1. The director should always perform as if he was actively campaigning. The museum directorship is, in essence, a political appointment; therefore the behavior of museum directors will have to follow the pattern of the average politician. The director will have to be prepared to project enthusiasm, interest and energy, promising all types of transformations and improvements within the institution, without ever committing to any plan in particular.

2. Directors will have the duty to censor exhibitions that they may deem inappropriate for their institution or offensive to the trustees. Nevertheless, they will have to be extremely careful to never address the censorship process as such. To be discovered in the process of censorship can initiate the end of a career. Good directors are known for their ability to disguise their censorship processes. A useful way to apply censorship to, as one example, an upcoming exhibition with problematic works is to change the premise of the exhibition in order to exclude the offensive works from the thematic context of the show.
3. The need will arise for the museum director to make special, implicit deals with sponsors in order to provide the museum with key financial and operational support. These secret contracts are known as "conflict of programming interests," of which the "donation" of money for an exhibition from a person who happens to be the owner or the author of the works is one. In these commonly occurring cases, the director must use maximum discretion. It is considered bad form for the director to give in to the pressure of the press and disclose the nature of the secret deal to the public, as this would be a disservice to the secret funder. For the institution, the disclosure would be catastrophic; on one hand the institution would lose the possibility of creating any future deals with future potential sponsors and on the other hand it would lose its credibility with the general public.
4. Directors will always foster the impression that they are aware of what is happening in their institutions. It is well known that directors are generally too busy with their social commitments to direct their museums, so it is acceptable for a director to delegate his everyday duties to one of his assistants, as long as he is careful not to break with the illusion that he himself is effectively behind every e-mail, every piece of correspondence, and omni-present within the institution.

The Collector

The collector's, or trustee's, position is the most enviable of them all, given that collectorship is not a profession but a hobby. Collectors are not subjected to pressure or influence by any part of the AW. Collectors perform their roles in an entirely free but not altogether disinterested manner; some do regard this activity as a professional sport and compete with other collectors.

Collectors rarely have any formal art background, and in general this background is not necessary for collecting, since they can be guided by specialists (curators or museum directors) who advise them in their shopping ventures. Nevertheless, collectors today have evolved from a passive to an active involvement in the AW. During the period up to the middle of the twentieth century, collectors would provide donations to institutions and would support artists by buying their work. Contemporary collectors are stockholders in a high-risk market where art comprises the collectors' portfolios. Considering that the acquisition of the work represents a financial risk, the collectors become directly involved in influencing the direction of the AW. An influential collector who puts up for sale all the works in his collection created by a certain artist would flood the market for these works, causing a drop in the prices of works by that artist.

On the other hand, given the collectors' economic and physical mobility, they are better exposed to artworks and artists. Being the main clients of galleries and museums, they are the ones with the greatest ability to pressure for the display of certain kinds of art. This is why it is understandable that non-material art (such as performance art or social experiments) is not greatly favored by the AW.

What makes a good collector/trustee? As in any sport, the collectors must succeed in the following: a) establishing a consistent quality of works in their collections; b) amply stocking those quality works; c) keeping and broadcasting a record of the number of works they have given or promised to give in the past; d) operating within a supportive family in order to ensure that the family will not fight a will bequeathing works to an institution; e) establishing a single institutional affiliation (a collector affiliated with more institutions dilutes the giving possibilities); f) avoiding interference with institutional agenda (it is preferable, in the best of all possible worlds, to have a collector who simply gives and refrains from attempting to run the institution's agenda, although most believe this restraint is now a thing of the past); g) refraining from developing curatorial aspirations (some collectors even attempt to curate—a big turnoff for institutions); and last but not least h) developing interest in hosting (collectors need to supply the entertaining for most social instances in the AW).

The following are a few etiquette musts for the good collector:

1. The collector must embrace his role and status in the AW. Some duties will involve attending boring board of trustee meetings, approving budgets, listening to the director's promotional speeches, attending openings, and hosting galas and opening parties for institutional sponsors.
2. Collectors must excel in their patience. They must understand that the AW in its entirety is in constant competition for their attention. At social events, even in instances where the collectors are not the least interested in someone's conversation, they will have to show courtesy to those who show them merchandise or invite them to social events.
3. The collector should not abuse his/her power in the AW by forcing curators, dealers and artists to see his/her personal family album, or forcing them to see each work in their collection, especially if the collection exceeds 4,000 works.
4. The collector must not be too cruel in the process of seducing a gallerist or artist by making the gallerist or artist believe that he is interested in them when he only wants to have fun.
5. Similarly, the collector must have certain regard toward dealers, curators and artists in social events that he/she organizes. All these people will feel obligated to attend the events, listen the collector's personal stories, and nod approvingly in response to everything the collector says, including the most passing thoughts, for as long as the collector speaks. It is important for the collector to realize that the reason that this entourage has been assembled is purely for work reasons: a similar situation is when the office boss subjects his employees to an interminable story of his family vacations. Collectors must understand that

their concerns, likely resulting from a comfortable position of money and privilege, are generally fairly incomprehensible, irrelevant, and superficial to others who are not able to partake in that kind of life.

6. Many collectors, when they start improving the quality of their collections, will begin to look into ways in which they can dispose of the works of certain artists who may not be "at the level" of the rest of the collection, especially those that perhaps were acquired at an early stage in their hobby. This activity, while essential, is extremely delicate and can cause the complete downfall of the artist's career. The collector will have to observe maximum discretion in the sale of unwanted work.
7. On some occasions, collectors who serve as trustees will have the opportunity to pressure the museum director to exhibit the works of the artists that comprise their personal collections in order to raise the value of this collection. It is unethical, nevertheless, to influence the museum to operate in such way without promising the donation of some works of this collection to the museum—or, alternatively, if the museum is not interested in those works, to offer money toward the construction of a new wing. Since the museum is risking its reputation by following these collectors' wishes, the individual collectors will also have to show their support.
8. It is recommended for collectors that, in order to acquire certain perspective on the situations of others, to take "reality courses." These courses have the objective of encouraging the collectors to imagine their lives without any kind of financial resource or security, having to live exclusively by their own talent. Because this experience can be extremely traumatic for most collectors, it is recommended they participate in these courses for three to four days at most.

The Collectors' Community

The collector, who generally is flattered and admired by all, has only one thing to fear: other collectors. Collectors compete only with each other. Collectors will be jealous of their respective territories and, like children who collect sports cards, will do everything possible to have the one artwork that everyone wishes to have. As a result, the collector should operate with care among his colleagues, give little information about his relationships with other institutions, and maintain friendly relations with all.

The Living Room Couch Crisis

Seasoned collectors will inevitably have to face the process of convincing their families (and particularly their spouses or life partners) to support each individual art purchase as well as their collecting hobbies in general. Among some of the traditional dilemmas faced by collectors, one of the greatest is acquiring a work that does not match with the living room's couch.

In this case, it will be the collector's responsibility to take certain precautions in order to not disappoint the artist or his/her wife/husband/partner. One of these precautions might be to budget allowing for purchase of additional living room couches to complement every artwork. In some cases, an additional living room can be built, or the work can be shipped to the winter home in Miami or San Diego.

Power Etiquette for the Culture Minister

In some countries where there is little collecting and the arts are usually subsidized by the state, the culture minister may play a very important role that is necessary to regulate here. We will define "culture minister" as that person with a government role that puts him/her in charge of directing the course of the arts policy in the country. The difference between the collector and the culture minister is that the collector has a financial, and sometimes fatally creative investment in the AW (when they convince institutions to show some of the untalented artists in their collections), while the culture minister has a political (and sometimes also fatally creative) investment in the AW. In most instances, the rules of the collector apply as well to the culture minister, with a few additions:

1. In order to maintain credibility, culture ministers should always claim to have experience in the visual arts, despite the fact that, according to recent data, only 1% of all culture

ministers have ever attended an art class. Additionally, they may discreetly take night courses and read self-help books (such as *Art for Dummies*, and this very manual) that will allow them to understand the intricacies of the AW. This will be particularly important if the culture minister has been designated as a result of being the spouse, friend or lover of an influential politician.

2. Culture ministers should not seek revenge on the AW's critiques of them by curating exhibitions or selecting spouses, friends or lovers as curators or artists for these exhibitions.
3. The culture minister should only attend the opening of exhibitions for the official portion of them, discreetly exiting after this. Choosing to remain at the event during the time allotted for excessive drinking and flamboyant behavior by the artists can only cause the party to lose excitement and energy.
4. In cases such as when the relative or lover of the culture minister calls her or himself an artist and demands a solo exhibition at the national gallery of the city or country, the culture minister should resist such pressures. Instead, the culture minister should further the art career of the relative or lover by securing them exhibitions at vanity galleries (as they will not notice the difference with an actual gallery).

The Curator

The responsibilities of the curator in the AW are of capital importance. The curator serves a moral, ethical, intellectual and sometimes parental role model for artists, and so must display exemplary behavior at all times. The curator is also the cultural, ideological and theoretical anchor of the AW. Being a curator is a great responsibility and those who excel in this practice will need to show great wisdom. On the other hand, the curator needs to develop sixth and seventh senses, both of which are critical to succeed. Their sixth sense lies in knowing which artists have the potential to be successful in the future, to the end of supporting their careers and being lauded as the "discoverer" of the artist. The seventh sense of the curator lies in knowing how to balance a curatorial agenda with interesting content, and both of these with the financial resources to make it happen. In other words, the curator must know how to translate complex contemporary art ideas into the simple language of the funder who is able to finance them.

Following are some key behavioral rules that need to be followed by a good curator:

1. Curators must have (or successfully pretend to have) knowledge of all the relevant artists working in the field. Lack of knowledge of any artist or of current events in the AW can indicate of lack of professionalism. This ignorance becomes, of course, more aggravating the more famous the referenced artist or events are. Occasionally, some influential curators will turn this rule to their advantage, pretending not to know a certain artist and by doing so creating the impression that this artist is of no relevance. Nevertheless, as a general rule, to admit that one doesn't know an artist while in a conversation during a social event can be a serious issue and embarrassing situation for a curator.
2. Curators should show knowledge of every subject and event that may attend their profession. Not doing so will only reflect badly on their professionalism. While in conversation, and when faced with a subject or event of which they are ignorant, curators must try to change the conversation, or nod ambiguously while the others present reference the subject or event. If asked directly whether one knows the artist or event, the curator should respond to the effect of "yes, I believe I have heard about this," leaving the impression that he or she was not sufficiently compelled by the subject to research further.
3. In the social environment, the curator must know how to use *namedropping strategies* (see the Glossary). Some curators can convincingly refer to famous artists using their first name, (e.g., "Matthew," "Cindy," "Jeff") with the intention to suggest closeness with his/her subjects.
4. Those curators who work for larger museums and institutions and who, in theory, are responsible for the artistic content of the institution, must learn to master the art of "thematic contextualization." The exhibitions organized by these institutions are generally decided by means beyond the power of the

curator, which is generally limited. This puts the curator in a compromising situation. In these cases, the curator cannot publicly acknowledge that the idea of any given exhibition was not his/her own since that would reveal his/her lack of power within the institution. So the curator is forced to generate a curatorial logic *a posteriori*, which would explain why the exhibition makes sense for the institution. Sometimes this "thematic contextualization" has to go to the end point of writing a catalogue essay for the exhibition.

5. Curators, like politicians, should keep a friendly attitude with all the artists. Regardless of how weak an artist may appear, it is in the curator's interest to show attention and sympathy to this artist, as one never knows who may eventually rise to stardom.

Feudal Principles

Curatorial society operates according to the medieval principle of the feudal lords. All curators should be aware that artists could effectively become their "territory" (although it is not desirable to let this be known to the artist, who needs to preserve his/her sense of freedom in order to create). The curator achieves importance in the AW in a manner that is directly proportional to the quantity of professional relationships he has developed with important artists. Curators who have not worked with important or famous artists have neither major relevance nor institutional weight. This is why it is important for a curator, as soon as possible, to begin having a stake in some artists' careers. A very effective strategy is to develop mass exhibitions with two hundred artists or more, which will exponentially expand the curator's possible pool of nascent art prodigies

The Unemployed Curator

Those curators who do not have an institutional job are normally known as *independent curators*. These curators do not have the attendant institutional obligations, but they are also subject nevertheless to "thematic contextualization" challenges. Independent curators may find themselves regularly facing the dilemma of having to work on projects that are not attractive or of particular relevance to their career, but which may be hard to turn down because they generate certain financial remuneration. In these cases, it is the curator's responsibility to make an effort and generate a convincing "thematic contextualization." Any deficiency in their performance will result in negative consequences for all involved. We must clarify also that independent curators must invest special efforts in showing extreme productivity, always making a new project both in order to show that their career is still alive and to sustain themselves financially (in contrast to institutional curators, who could very easily work on a single project for many years). The independent curator will then need to make an effort to disguise the pressures of his job, and instead of showing off his/her excess of projects (which may only make him/her appear overextended) will have to project an image of control and selectivity.

The Art Consultant

Other curators in similar situation operate as "art consultants." Art consultants, like independent curators, do not have an institutional position but they adapt their practice to become a hybrid between a curator and a dealer. Art consultants make deals with galleries and specialize in forging friendships with collectors who are extremely rich and extremely ignorant about art in order to help them decorate their residences. It is the duty of the art consultant to dress extremely well, in order to compensate their lack of institutional affiliation, and have a profound knowledge of upper class life in order to converse fluently with collectors, thereby gaining their trust. It is of utmost importance for art consultants to have a grasp of interior design and be subscribed to *Martha Stewart Living.*

Regional Curators

Also more or less within the genre of unemployed art experts, those curators who feel disenfranchised by the AW and live in small cities or countries can always find a job in the mainstream by positioning themselves as "regional" curators. A curator living in a peripheral community can hardly manage to curate a show on a universal topic, but will always be given opportunities to talk about his/her immediate surroundings. Curators who work in this field, which is a modality of the feudal principle, will discover that there will be few attempts by the AW to challenge their definitions and theories about this region. We only advise these curators to avoid developing overly bitter feelings and resentments toward the community that will also provide their daily thematic and monetary subsistence.

The Curator as Artistic Director

A popular form of exercising the curatorial position is to adopt the commonly known strategy, once invented by Harald Szeemann, of becoming the "artistic-curatorial director." The artistic-curatorial director generates curatorial and/or artistic ideas *a priori* and later proceeds to find artists that will fit within these themes. The artistic-curatorial director has the advantage of not having to spend time researching or paying attention to the common themes that concern contemporary artists, since all the ideas for the curator's exhibitions will come exclusively from his imagination. The practice today is very effective thanks to the overflow in the artist supply market. It is never difficult to find groups of artists who may generate work according to any theme or premise. This process of generating exhibitions can be greatly entertaining for the curator.

Artistic Ventriloquists

The artistic-curatorial-director position can evolve into other positions. Some of these practitioners become known as *artistic ventriloquists.* These are curatorial-artistic-directors who have developed a team of artists who virtually function as their assistants, being sufficiently eager to implement any of the curator's ideas, going out to the world to make them happen, and turning into a sort of representative of the curator's aesthetic theories. Those curators who act as artistic ventriloquists generally seek to establish a true international influence as theorists.

It is important to note that the artistic ventriloquist technique can be also applied by artists who may want to have certain influence in the field, nurturing a group of followers of greater or lesser talent (be it other artists or curators). The lesser talents in any case, will act as truthful followers of the artistic ventriloquist and will be obedient and flexible regarding the thematic directives of the artist. It is unnecessary to enumerate all the advantages of such a relationship; essentially, the followers will be offered special career opportunities, while the ventriloquist will benefit by creating a support group and a historic legacy. Artists in academia can greatly benefit from this system, making extensions of their careers in the lives of their students.

The Speculating Curator

The experienced curator can begin to generate even more sophisticated strategies while interacting with the AW. Some of the most aggressive curators are known as *curators-speculators*. The curator-speculator uses a support base that may include a relationship with a gallery, and, through the credibility provided by his/her supposedly objective position, can secretly support the artists with whom this gallery works. Eventually the curator-speculator will benefit financially from the revenues that the rise as the reputation of (and the price of artworks by) the artist rises. Of course, if these practices become public, the curator-speculator will lose the ability to maneuver, and so it is recommended that the curator-speculator exercise extreme care and discretion in this activity.

On Curatorial Puberty

While curatorial precociousness is a somewhat recent phenomenon initiated by Hans Ulrich Obrist, it is not a guaranteed route for young curators. In general, while youth can be advantageous in the contemporary art field, it is difficult to gain respect in the AW when one is only beginning an institutional career.

Young curators who wish to succeed will have to follow certain strategic forms of behavior:

1. The young curator must find an influential mentor, preferably a curator of international recognition. These curators are generally in need of curatorial assistants who will do their work, so that they themselves can travel around the world to meet their daily social commitments. Those young curators who have the opportunity to assist the curatorial luminary must never complain about the amount of work and their lack of recognition—instead, they need to keep quiet and work ex-

tremely hard. Their dedication will ensure that their mentor will keep them in mind in the future and will pay them back with substantial contacts and recommendations.

2. The young curator will have to compete with other young curators for the role of "promising new young curator," normally available in certain institutions or in certain countries. The competition will be rather unpleasant, but necessary. At all times though, the curator should pretend not to be competing with anyone but directing his/her efforts to working.

In Bed with the Artist

It is fairly common for curatorial assistants to be in charge of the schedule and travel logistics of international artists who may come to visit institutions in order to mount their artworks. This usually also results in brief flings, one-night stands, and even longstanding affairs. It is not recommended for young curators to sleep with famous artists, since the rumors can be greatly damaging for the young curator's career. If one must have an affair of this sort, the young curator should be extremely secretive and under no circumstance brag about it to coworkers. On the other hand, if this relationship has taken place, the curatorial assistant should enjoin the famous artist to offer favors and opportunities such as job recommendations, since the established artists can be extremely helpful in this regard.

Overcoming Power "Highs"

It is a common tendency of the young curator to become inebriated with the power that the name of "curator" carries, especially if one works at an important institution. Immediately, the young curator will receive excessive attention in his/her social surroundings, inducing the young curator to speak more than necessary. This gives the impression that he/she has more influence within the institution than he/she does (which at the beginning is normally nonexistent). While the curatorial assistant can initially use these impressions to his/her advantage, these can become dangerous if they reach the ears of his/her supervisor.

How to Milk Successful Artists

The common wisdom is that within the artist-curator relationship it is the curator who has the advantage. In reality, as the artist becomes well known, he/she can gain control of the curators with whom he/she works, while for curators it becomes more prestigious to work with an already recognized artist. One of the greatest fortunes for a curator is to cement a strong relationship with an important artist. This relationship will eventually give the curator a strong card to play in his/her career. The recognized artist will have to be conscious of the importance of favoring certain curators rather than others, and would have to be careful not to abuse them.

A Note on Curatorial Fencing

In the same fashion as artists, the curatorial profession is highly competitive. Therefore, it is even more important to maintain a good relationship with curatorial colleagues. Curators must be aware that their colleagues will be possessive about certain artists with whom they have worked in the past. When a curator begins working with an artist (especially if it is a famous one) the relationship can generate jealousy in other curators, and turn them into enemies. Given this case, if a curator A organizes an exhibition of an artist with whose work a curator B has worked on and/or considers himself/herself specialist, it is good etiquette for curator A to invite curator B to write an essay for the exhibition catalogue. If this does not happen, curator B will have every right to exclude curator A from every future project where curator A could potentially collaborate, and B could even begin organizing exhibitions with artists who belong in the territory of curator A. The curator B will also be free to spread the word within the curatorial community about curator A's lack of teamwork, so that no one works with him/her again.

Psychological Etiquette

Many curators believe that, given their influence in their field, they have the right to modify the work of the artists. For example, they may suggest changes in the format of the works, in the coloring, in the materials, in the topics, in the manufacture and so on; or they may manufacture mistakes and so on. Many artists are more than eager to satisfy such requests in order to please the curators. Nevertheless, these kinds of acts often generate a kind of uncomfortable dependency of the artist on the curator. If the curators are not careful, soon the artists will come to them on a regular basis to help resolve and approve every project. If a curator wishes to influence the production of his or her artists, the psychological strategies below are most effective:

1. The artist/curator relationship is of a "professional love affair." For this reason, the curator should never reveal to the artist any preference for another artist. While the process of seduction is much easier from the curator to the artist than in reverse, the curator must be careful not to take the artist's "love" for granted. The curator must keep the artist away from any other conversations he or she may have with other artists. This would cause only jealousy and resentment in the artist, the seriousness of the curator's intentions will be called into question.
2. In many instances, a curator will invite an artist to an exhibition for reasons that are exclusive of the value of the artist's work (such as, for example, needing gender, racial or geographic diversity; or because a better artist declined to participate). In these cases, the curator should never reveal to the artist the real reasons for the invitation, stressing only the value of the artist's work.
3. When a curator wants to include in the exhibition a particular work that is not the one that the artist favors, the curator should employ a persuasion technique based in flattery (for example, "this would definitely be the best work in the show") or envy ("I rather show your work than X's, because he has a very similar work to this one but it is not as effective.") The

strategy should function, to allow the artist himself to conclude that the best work to show, his own, is the one that the curator had intended from the beginning.

4. In the case of artists whose artistic peak has passed, the curator would normally want to include works that correspond to their best period. The artist, in contrast, will generally want to show new work, which will almost always not be at the same level as the earlier work. The curator will then have to use all his talent to convince the artist that his "historical" work would help contextualize the exhibition, presenting the artist in the light of a seminal figure.
5. The curator should always leave the door open to the artist, making the artist believe that this is only one of many future invitations to exhibit. The artist in this way will remain permanently in expectation to these invitations, allowing the curator the position of advantage.

Google as a Curatorial Tool

One of the greatest challenges among curators is to maintain productivity within the AW, each generating many exhibition ideas and essays. Search engines can provide a great relief in this respect if one follows strategies such as the following:

1. In order to generate quick exhibition ideas: a) open a dictionary and point a finger to any page randomly; b) take the "selected" word as the topic of the exhibition and search Google using this word along with the phrase "contemporary art"; c) generate a preliminary artist list based on the names that will come up from the mentioning of this subject. For instance, if the random word is "animal," the search should provide a list of artists who use animals in their work (e.g., Joseph Beuys, Diana Thater).
2. In order to write an essay on any subject, type the theme of the essay alongside the word "conceptual." The search results will also work as bibliography.
3. In order to complete any published project, doing an interview with the artist will prove the most efficient and useful method.

Interviews are greatly popular since they help the curator to avoid taking a direct stance on any subject, remain as the questioner, and place the burden on the artist to come up with the "answers." Additionally, interviews can be completed in a few minutes and result in many pages of text that can be edited by curatorial assistants.

Commercial Etiquette: Dealers and Their Galleries

Contemporary art dealership is probably the most difficult occupation in the AW, and perhaps the least socially attractive after the critic's—although it clearly is the most profitable. A gallery is first and foremost a business, but one subject to variables, such as the changes of taste, the good or bad career luck of the gallery artists, and the ups and downs of the art market, that usually are out of the dealer's hands. It would seem logical for many dealers to give up selling such a volatile product and instead sell goods in consistent demand and with consistent value. But of course, the dealer's job is critical to the AW and we all should be deeply appreciative of those who have to bridge the uncomfortable gap between the incalculable spiritual value of art and its objective commercial value.

Following are a few etiquette guidelines for the dealer, inspired by the example of those who have succeeded in this field.

1. As it happens with dog owners in New York, the gallery's appearance mirrors its owner's, and vice versa. This rule will be self-evident to any art dealer, as well as to any regular gallery visitor. A dirty gallery should not be tolerated, nor should any space not immaculate and entirely neutral. A lack of cleanliness will not only be a reflection of the lack of sophistication of the dealer, but it will also show a lack of respect for the visitor.
2. One must remember that contemporary art is frequently uncomfortable to watch and of questionable moral value. So it is essential for the space to look pristine and elegant. The gallery should project a neutral harmony. Some dealers hire feng shui specialists in order to bring "good flow of energy" into the space. This is recommended. It is not good form to

hang garlic at the entrance of the spaces nor to perform any acts of Santeria; while these objects may scare the bad spirits away, they may also scare potential buyers who do not believe in these practices, as well as those rich collectors who may not always have good spirits in them.

3. The previous rules can be ignored if the gallery is trying to use dirt and an ugly neighborhood as an aesthetic statement, leaving the peeling paint on the walls, illuminating the rusting industrial pipes, and even strategically fitting an aquarium into one of the gallery walls. European collectors are fond of this look particularly when the gallery is located in places like Williamsburg, Brooklyn or any rough, undeveloped neighborhood. Nevertheless, these design decisions have their limitations, and must be abandoned once the gallery moves to Chelsea.
4. Dealers will need to dress in an immaculate manner, preferably with a colorful and elegant English cut shirt and sports jacket during regular business days for men, and black dresses for women. The dealer will also have to adjust his or her clothing accordingly when attending social events like the Venice Biennial by dressing in white with dark glasses. For dealers who are *not* gay (who also are those in greatest need of fashion advice), it is recommended to wear a sober and uncomfortable suit that reflects the character of the gallery. In the case of assistants, it is recommended to hire attractive men and women between 20 and 23 years of age with women dressed in black and revealing tops, and the men wearing tight nylon black shirts. Hiring assistants with an elegant foreign accent is very helpful. Many contemporary art sales analyses reveal that collectors, generally white Caucasian men, older than 40 and half of them gay, respond favorably to the visual attraction of the gallery assistant, which makes them more likely to purchase art.
5. It is preferable for the owner of the gallery not to be seen at all, hiding behind closed doors. This way, important clients will appreciate the special treatment when they are taken through the door to the back office. However, in most cases the dealer may need to have his or her desk on view in the gallery. If this is the

case, the dealer must never be seen inactive. He or she will always need to be, if not at a meeting, speaking on the phone or working at the computer. If the dealer is seating numbly at the desk at a moment when the visitor arrives, he or she should immediately begin showing some activity, even if by making an imaginary phone call. If the visitor is a prominent person, the dealer will interrupt this activity immediately, thus showing his or her deference to the visitor. If the visitor is a random, average person, the imaginary activity will help the dealer to establish a symbolic shield from interaction with the proletarian art audience.

Designing a Gallery with Taste

For those dealers who are already successful and have managed to create galleries with international reputation, it is recommended to use the architectural design style known as "Mary Boone," in acknowledgement of its originator. This design strategy consists of situating a stainless-steel reception desk at the entrance of the gallery, at which is seated a severe-looking assistant in front of a tall shelf with scrupulously arranged binders.

Although some critics—perhaps out of jealousy—have nicknamed this gallery style "Eighties Neo-Nazi," it is undeniable that such design communicates power and credibility, inspiring respect in the viewer.

Gallery Dress Code

At art fairs, the art dealer will have to display his or her personal style with the greatest care, in order to distinguish him or herself from the endless array of dealers. It is recommended not to try to be too original—costuming oneself as a penis, for instance, if requested by one of the conceptual artists of the gallery to do so, or displaying one's breasts through a see-through dress.

Art dealers must be educated about and considerate of all those who enter their gallery, and should make them feel at home. This can become one of the greatest social challenges for the art dealer, who instead of investing time in wooing potential buyers will have to dedicate a quantity of time and attention to inexperienced artists with slides in hand and looking for gallery representation (and who usually appear at the exact time when the most important collector enters the gallery) or to elderly women without any buying interest and who only are in search of conversation. In these instances, the art dealer must learn to show interest in any kind of conversation.

The Slight Arrogance as Virtue

When facing the potential buyer, the professional art dealer will need to learn how to develop a commercial behavior that will not present him or her as subservient to the buyer. An overly helpful attitude will be interpreted as lack of experience or extreme desperation to sell work. The dealer should show a bit of arrogance and even a slight disdain, as if he or she were giving the collector permission to enter into his or her space. This will be apprehended by the collector as an indication that the gallery is a social club to which he or she wishes to belong.

Art Fair Behavior

One of the most difficult abilities for an art dealer to develop is *spatial omnipresence*, particularly during an art fair. Art fairs move very quickly, and rental spaces are so expensive that one needs to maximize every second of available time and not to lose a single sale opportunity. The art dealer who masters this technique will be able to intercept any potential sale by having absolute visual and aural awareness of the activity within his or her booth without turning his or her head in a conspicuous manner. This allows the art dealer to have a conversation with a person while simultaneously keeping track of the conversation of a potential couple of collectors at the other end of the booth. Art dealers with experience can be in this way involved in four simultaneous transactions, and talking to as many as six simultaneous clients while giving the impression that they are solely dedicated to each one of them.

While participating in the art fair, the dealer must be master of the art of innocuous conversation. It is completely forbidden for the dealer to make any sort of negative comments during these interactions. The art dealer may commiserate with visitors about topics such as the weather, the annoyances of travel at the airport, the local cuisine, etc., but in no instance may the dealer critique his or her competition in public nor, more importantly, speak about his or her gallery's financial problems.

At all times he or she must project that things are going excellently well, that all the work is sold out and that there is great demand for more.

Facing Adversity

The average art dealer will go through difficult financial, and other, situations. Nevertheless, dealers should never cease projecting a successful image, even if their business is on the brink of collapse. It is recommended that the dealer face his or herself at the mirror right after waking up every morning, and in complete privacy, repeat: "I am the next Larry Gagosian" or "I am the next Barbara Gladstone."

The Artist

At the dawn of modernism, artists worked hard in their studios, usually in isolation, suffering all kinds of deprivations, until they would be discovered by a dealer or taken on by a patron, critic or curator. Nowadays, artistic suffering has not vanished, but its nature has changed. Art-school-produced, professional artists spend less time in a studio, but rather live a nomadic life between airports, recovering from jetlag brought on by their endless transits between residencies, biennials, art fairs, speaking engagements, openings and other social events. Professional artists accomplish more work on their laptops and via e-mail than at the studio. They must also attend interminable dinners with eccentric collectors and spend all-nighters filling out grant proposals.

Truly successful artists are the ones who recognize that their traditional art school education has proved completely useless and proceed to develop practical skills such as digital programming, ethnography and sociology, perceptual psychology, business administration, industrial and product design, marketing, architecture and engineering.

The way artists' manner of rising to the top is also changed. While in the past artists were selected by a small group of *connoisseurs* who were educated about art history, today the artists can achieve recognition when supported by those of wealth and willingness promote their work. Artists should be willing to work with their supporters to continue manufacturing products in accordance with demands and in response to artistic market trends.

There is a general, if unspoken, gradation hierarchy for artists that is based on international and institutional recognition. Although it is never publicly acknowledged, this hierarchy is a useful reference for those who wish to sense the location of certain artists (including, perhaps, themselves) within the professional landscape of the AW.

A-level (also known as "blue-chip") artists are generally those who participate with regularity in the main international biennials, whose work is owned by major museum collections, and who are regularly written about in *Artforum*. The A-level status is difficult to maintain on a long-term, even less on a permanent, basis. All artists claim to be A-level artists. An A-level status can be held for as little as one week in the AW. A-level artists constitute the top 3% of the market.

B-level artists are those who occasionally exhibit in international biennials and do have works in some significant collections, but whose exhibition and review record is uneven. Approximately 15% of the AW is comprised of B-level artists.

C-level artists, usually known as "emerging" artists, can be identified as follows: a) their career is in its very early stages; b) they never managed to quite take off despite several attempts; c) they were previously A- or B-level artists but, after a decline in their careers, refused to give up making art. C-level artists can have a handful of significant exhibitions on record, but not enough to justify a B-level rating. Around 32% of the artists involved in the AW belong to this group.

D-level artists are generally amateurs with naïve awareness of the AW and with little critical judgment about their own work. They are generally regarded as hopeless and constitute 50% of the market.

Artists will rarely succeed if they do not observe basic rules of professional behavior, proactive actions, and passive strategies that are outlined here. The following rules will allow aspiring artists to develop strong relationships, to create a support basis, and to hide the ugliness of their artistic ambition behind a likable or magnetic personality.

1. *Appearances in society.* Artists' appearances at public events such as openings will be inversely proportional to the success of the artist's career—with the possible exception, of course, of the artists' own openings. Artists who attend too many openings will inevitably generate suspicion about the seriousness of their artistic intentions.

2. *Physical Appearance.* Artists must attempt, at all times, to have an interesting appearance, one that implies great introspective and psychological intensity. Being physically attractive is most desirable, but in case of not having such attributes, an artist must develop "character." Artists should dress keeping up with fashion, adding an unexpected element (for example, colored socks). Such an element will send the message that, while the artist is able to conform to the rules of the game, he or she is still able to provide an artistic, individual vision. One should be cautious not to overdo a look, as it may backfire, creating the impression that one has an adolescent desire for attention.
3. *Conversation.* At the opening, the artist should not initiate any conversation by saying that he or she is an artist, but rather should be patiently quiet, as if taking for granted that the people in the party know who he or she is. In any group with minimum decency, someone will surely ask about his or her profession, which will then be the cue to begin talking.
4. *Plug-in.* This term is applied to the artist's strategy of promoting his or her work during a passing-by commentary, such as "the other day, as I was coming out of the studio with the curator of Sao Paulo's biennial . . ."etc. Through the *plug-in* method, the artist can easily establish his or her stature without sounding too pretentious. The plug-in must be inserted in a casual tone, which will create the impression that the artist is used to high-level experiences and opportunities.
5. *Hyper-self-aggrandizement.* Those artists who may want to have a strong impact in the AW should value themselves excessively—for example, asking that their work be transported by the most expensive art shipping company, or/and that they be given business class tickets along with their assistants. While the artist may sometimes be scorned for this attitude, in reality his or her status will definitely rise in the AW, causing controversy and, in some cases, admiration. The attitude of the artist in this case will need to be at all times that of someone who sees his or her importance not as a debatable point but as an undeniable fact—which will make his or her stature even more convincing. Those artists of low self-esteem or weak personality are cautioned against employing this technique.

In their cases, using hyper-self-aggrandizement may result in self-deception, making the artist convince him or herself of the fictional value he or she has promoted. This can lead to traumatic situations when the artist encounters situations where his or her true value becomes apparent—such as not being invited to certain exhibitions, openings, dinners, etc.

6. *Hyper-humility*. In the case of famous artists, however, hyper-self-aggrandizement can be redundant and counterproductive, since it will only alienate those admirers who normally surround this artist. As a strategy to counter the last point, the famous artist should practice *hyper-humility*. Hyper-humility is very attractive because it helps people to relax when they feel intimidated by the artist's fame. Hyper-humility works like a false modesty, but it requires flawless performance in order to hide its falsehood and make it convincing. Hyper-humble artists, for example, should act with surprise when someone expresses interest about their work, as if this were a rarity. When the artist is flattered or offered a certain distinction, he/she should act as if this was undeserved.

Choosing Friends and Partners

Value by association (best summarized by the saying "tell me who you are with and I will tell you who you are") has always been true in the AW and it is vital to consider the importance of this concept in this manual. Because the AW generally works by first (and visual) impressions and instinct more than by fully rational considerations, offering a strong first image of oneself is essential. Here we enumerate some basic procedures, which are valid both for artists as well as for anyone who wishes to give a favorable impression.

1. It is essential that one associate exclusively with those who are at a higher professional level than oneself. Only in this way can an art professional aspire to ascend the social ladder and to rise in the field. In contrast, those who surround themselves with less successful people will be associated with their position within the AW. The successful artist, additionally, should look for counterparts in other fields, visiting exhibitions, for

example, with singers, movie stars, designers and models, all of those being public positions that carry much greater *cache* than the AW itself.

2. A constant question in the AW is: should one sleep with an artist whose work one does not like? The response to this, a resounding no, is not too easy to follow through. The dynamic of the AW, with its extremely social environment of evening receptions and parties makes it easy to forget any sort of AW standards. As well, it is undeniable that many extremely attractive people may also be bad artists. Our recommendation is that, even though it may appear inevitable to submit every now and then to our sexual impulses, it is of utmost importance to remember that this may cause serious damage to the general perception of our positions within the AW.
3. As a result of the previous discussion, it is a common—and unfortunate—scenario to see a successful artist or curator accompanied by a mediocre partner, hopelessly competing for attention while being in the shadow of her or his more successful partner. To those successful artists who have the tendency choose partners who are 20 years younger than they, common advice is not to make any efforts to promote the career of this person, or use evident strategies to impose their partner's work onto the opportunities that are presented to them (for example, making collaborative works or exhibitions). It is important to remember that even in the visual arts love is always blind.
4. For those whose partners, formerly of the same position, experience a sudden career take-off toward fame, it is recommended that the less successful partner either abandon his or her original career or, if he or she desires to persist in his or her profession, abandon the relationship altogether. The AW society usually shies away at the sight of a successful artist next to another who has not been equally successful. Nevertheless, when this situation is inevitable, the artist's admirers will be obliged to support the career of his or her partner if he or she requests so. While, as we said before, it is inappropriate for the artist to request support from his or her partner, the supporters of the famous artist will have to be sensitive to the famous artist's ordeal and must try to aid in the situation, as

difficult as this may be. Even though any project done by the partner will likely not be very good and sometimes altogether not transcendental, supportive behavior on the part of any outside artist, dealer or curator will make the famous artist happy, which is what really matters in this situation.

Regarding Friendships with Artists

Several instances are known of which artists, apart from being good creative minds, are also admirable in the art of friendship. The main limitation of an artist is his or her lack of generosity and inability to relate to or even want to listen to the problems of others, all of which is essential virtue in a friend. Much, however, can be achieved by keeping in mind that an artist will always want to be listened to at least three times more than a normal person.

Artists and Galleries

As we have discussed in regards to the curator, the relationship between the artist and the dealer has the elements of a seductive courtship, and later, of a pact similar to marriage. For those familiar with the initial process, it is clear when the initial courtship process is in vain. Some inexperienced artists may persist in trying to develop a relationship for years without realizing that they have not the slightest hope to show the gallery of their "friend." Once the appropriate and reciprocating gallery is found, both the artist and the art dealer must enter into the agreement that, however formal, will never cease either to be a little uncomfortable or to have certain instability. It is fair for either the gallery or the artist to "drop" the other when presented with a better opportunity at any time.

For the artist seeking gallery representation, it is important to observe the following rules:

1. The artist should never enter a gallery with slides in hand and the purpose of showing them to the dealer "if a chance arises." This strategy is commonly known as the "insurance salesman" strategy. Artists should also not enter the gallery with artworks, especially if they are oversized.

2. An artist who enters a gallery for the first time without having seen the previous exhibitions or even the show on view, and who walks directly to the desk and tries to drop off his or her slides and curriculum vitae, is showing grave disrespect to the gallery. If the artist has not even bothered to examine the program of the gallery, why should the dealer invest any time in reviewing the work of the artist? Although this manual does not encourage it, it is understandable that in those instances, some dealers will take the slides, in front of the artist, and put them directly into the trash.
3. European artists who come to New York galleries should not bring copies of their catalogues. It is well known that in Europe anyone can afford to print a catalogue, and to bring one along with slides usually causes envy from those galleries that rarely can afford to produce any publication.
4. Artists should not harass the galleries by first sending their unsolicited slides and later calling the gallery in order to ask for the materials back, via Federal Express.
5. Artists should be cautioned that dealers will rarely be cordial when solicited. If an artist enters a gallery in a place like New York and is cordially greeted, and asked whether one is an artist, the artist should be put on guard and suspect immediately that the place may be a "vanity gallery" (see glossary).

Invoicing Etiquette

It is unfortunately a common problem that a gallery sells a work or works and waits a disproportionate amount of time before either informing the artist of the sale or giving out the percentage due to the artist. It is not recommended for the artist to sue, given that the gallery will likely have better legal and financial resources. More effective is to contact the gallery's clients to inform them of the murky financial practices of the gallery. In extreme cases of gallery abuse, rules no longer apply.

On Curatorial Guardian Angels

The artist-curator relationship, perhaps the most complex in the AW, has partially been discussed in the curatorial section. Artists should review that section in order to be aware of the curatorial guidelines that will be applied to them, so that they can be prepared to observe them. The artist should also follow these guidelines:

1. The artist should do whatever possible to make the curator feel comfortable in the interactions between them, and in control of their discursive dynamic. Any attempt by the artist to question the curator's premises, as absurd as these may be, may intimidate the curator and damage the relationship over time.
2. Artists should always appear to show interest in the ideas of the curator.
3. The artist must master the art of improvisation. If, for example, the artist is attending a social gathering and comes across a curator and the curator mentions an exhibition he or she is organizing on a certain topic, the artist should immediately mention that he or she is currently addressing the same topic in his or her work.
4. An artist should never complain or place any demands on the curator. The artist will always be in debt to the curator and, as badly as any given exhibition may turn out, it is in the interest of the artist to be quiet and avoid any conflict rather than risking the possibility of being invited to participate in future projects.

Death Duels: Artist vs. Artist

1. An artist is, essentially, the competition of other artists. Art history does not allow much space for artists of the same period and place, so what concerns artists of the same generation, nationality, and social status is that sooner or later one or the other will take the available place.
2. Nevertheless, it is important that artists not reveal their jealousy, resentments or irritation when they may see a colleague receiv-

ing an opportunity that they would rather receive themselves. In order to minimize these aggravations, the AW has wisely devised a series of unspoken rules that keep a minimum appearance of courtesy among artists, especially for those who live in the same community.

3. When two artists belonging more or less to the same geographic or stylistic environment or community meet for the first time, they should introduce themselves by their first names, assuming that the other person already knows them and "has seen the work." The encounter between these two artists must be of a reserved character; like in poker, the players in this context need to keep their cards close to themselves.
4. In larger AW capitals like New York, London or Berlin, the relationship between artists tends to be more relaxed since opportunities are more varied and available. Nevertheless, the artists will have to become familiar with the advanced methods of networking: a) always ending exchanges that occur during openings and receptions by offering business cards and, if one is to have an exhibition soon, 4×6" postcards available with the information regarding the exhibition; b) being abreast of all the artistic events of the city; c) always "having something to offer" to other artists—for example, some sort of curatorial contact, information of a certain scholarship, residency, etc. As with trading card exchanges, this initiative must be reciprocated by most artists.

What to Do with Imitators?

It is not unusual for an artist to encounter a colleague whose works have ideas, artistic process and physical appearances that may be suspiciously similar to his or her own. Nonetheless, coincidental thinking has its limits, and while imitators are well known for making one believe that they are capable of generating revelatory ideas, more often than not the original artist knows for a fact that these works are merely "rip-offs" from his or her creations. This practice, known as "plagiarism," is as old as art itself, and there are a variety of solutions, from public embarrassment and legal action to even murder. This manual does not recommend the more extreme measures but rather the more subtle techniques mentioned below:

1. Imitated artists will have to hide their anger about the forgery incident, which, in most cases, will be hard to prove. Instead, the imitated artist should warmly thank their colleague for having made a work that "pays homage" to the imitated artist.
2. Immediately following, the imitated artist should ensure that the whole AW knows about this "homage." This strategy will certify that the work is recognized as a forgery before being mistakenly acknowledged as an original piece, thus humiliating the imitator and securing the original's position in the AW.
3. In the case that the forger or imitator may claim innocence or ignorance, or accuses the imitated artist of jealousy, the artist will then have the right to claim the forged work as his or her own. If the imitated work is for sale, the imitated artist will have the right to demand 25% of the sale price of the work, given that this percentage represents the content of the work that belongs to the original artist.
4. If the forger/imitator still refuses to admit plagiarism, the imitated artist should then invest in hiring three young art student assistants whose purpose will be to make even worse replicas of the works made by the forger. The hired imitators should then sign the works with the forger's name, and introduce them to the market over the course of two or three years. The original artist will ensure that every time he or she makes an original work and it has been seen and exhibited, that the supposedly "forged" work made by his or her assistants is also seen a few weeks later. After some short time, the forger's reputation as a forger and bad artist will be firmly established.

Scratching the Other's Back: the Art of Reciprocity

Professional artists know that the knowledge or influence of even their greatest enemies can benefit them in some way as long as one is willing to participate in a reciprocal exchange of information regarding such subjects as grants, useful contacts, and tips. The art of reciprocity can only be mastered by practice. When engaging in an exchange, it is preferable to initiate it by offering a small favor, tip, or hint to another artist. Once this is done, the other artist must reciprocate. If the other artist does not reciprocate, one should stop providing information altogether.

An artist should never be overly generous with information if he or she is not be able to get the same in return, nor should the artist be overly secretive, since this will discourage those who may be able to exchange information.

Attending the Openings of Others

The art of reciprocity and exchange does not operate exclusively on the basis of sharing information, but also on the more tangible level of attending the openings of other artists, with the main objective of generating attendance to one's own opening when the time comes.

If an artist 1 attends the opening of artist 2, it will be the duty of artist 2 to attend the opening of artist 1. In fact, it is the ethical duty of every artist and curator to attend the openings of all of those artists and curators of note who attend their openings. If one does not follow this rule, it is certain that attendance levels of one's exhibitions will decline considerably. Attending openings can be seen as an investment in oneself. In terms of opening attendance reciprocity, there is a tolerance of missing some events, but this wears thin as soon as it is perceived that the artist is making excuses and is not supporting colleagues.

When There Is No Time to Make Art

It often happens to some artists who observe the previous rules very strictly that their social agenda (e.g., attending openings) will make it impossible for them to make art.

This condition is often diagnosed as *openingitis,* the chronic addiction to attending openings. If one wishes to recover from this condition, it is useful to announce an absence from the city for an extended period of time, which becomes a good pretext not to appear at openings. In those cases, one should just be careful not to walk around familiar AW neighborhoods, since one may be seen and be caught in deceit. If one, however, discovers that it is more enjoyable for them to attend openings than actually make any art, he or she may be able to pull off an *artist-socialite* career, which is the one pursued by artists who do not in fact make any work at the studio but instead pose as artists at openings, telling imaginary stories about the work they do and the exhibitions they produce.

The Artist's Nemesis: The Critic

There are few occasions on which the artist will have less defensive power than when interacting with the critics. The relationship between the artist and the critic is extremely fragile, and entirely dependent on the temperament of the critic. In the case that the critic becomes irritated by the constant self-promotional harassment of the artist, the result can be catastrophic for the latter. The critic, like an irritated bee, can sting, and sting painfully. For that reason, it is recommended to maintain an arm's length distance from the critic and to not pursue any relationship not initiated by the critic himself. During openings, the artist should say a brief hello to the critic and be as friendly as possible, but not try to seduce him to her or start a self-promotional speech. In general, it is preferable to have a mediator between the artist and the critic, such as a curator or an art dealer.

The one exception to this rule applies to the "critics for hire," in which case the relationship between the critic and the artist will change. The "critics for hire" (see the Critic section) are those who are hired by the artist or his or her gallery to write an essay about the exhibition for the catalogue (a less ethical practice is when the gallery pays the critic to write a favorable critique for a magazine). In these cases, the dialogue is more relaxed and the power relationship becomes more leveled.

Aside from this one exception, artists should be always ready to face the worst in terms of criticism. It is useful to remember that art criticism was not invented to provide new insights into art, but rather to take new insights brought by artists and curators and prove that they are not new, good enough, or well formulated enough. Artists should regard themselves as a cultivated field that is harvested by the critics, or in some cases, a forest that needs to be regularly burned down to the ground in order to be cultivated again.

The Artist in Self-Intimacy

Artists often believe that it is their behavior in public that will be the most critical to their success. In fact, there is nothing more critical than their behavior while in total solitude. It is common knowledge that the artist job has no schedule. True artists should always perform like artists, particularly when they are alone. This practice will first strengthen the artist's personality for public performance times, and will ensure that the artist will not be caught off-guard in front of any inconspicuous surveillance or closed-circuit camera.

1. In a similar fashion to the art dealer's self-affirmation morning exercises, the artist should also look at him or herself in the mirror every morning and, in a loud and clear voice, and without laughter, convincingly proclaim him or herself to be the most important artist in history. If the artist does not maintain such conviction, any efforts to truly succeed will undoubtedly end in failure.
2. Artists should show an unconditional love for themselves. Without unconditional self-love and admiration, it will be very difficult for an artist to be loved by others as well. Additionally to this self-love, artists should also ensure to reciprocate their love for themselves.
3. Artists should do daily "originality exercises" in order to increase charisma and enrich their personalities. Such exercises will consist of doing common activities in unusual ways, such as squeezing the toothpaste in an original way, using kitchen utensils for gardening, cooking with art tools, etc.
4. Artists should be prepared always for any unannounced visitor by placing strange and exotic objects in their living environments and studios, so that these places appear original.
5. Artists should beware of competing against themselves. Often, artists past their prime will become resentful toward the works they produced in the past. As artists age, they must be careful not to criticize their own early career. It is better to be recognized for something that one did a long time ago than not be recognized for anything at all.

The Media Persona

Artists should attempt to dedicate ample time and efforts to expanding the originality of their ideas, their outfits, their vocal affectations, and even their way of walking—all of which will make them a more desirable media target. Speaking clearly works to no avail with the press, which inevitably distorts their well-chosen words. Therefore, it is desirable for any artist to respond to interviews with enigmatic comments or even better, answer questions with new questions. This way, artists will ensure that their comments are never clear enough to be simplified, and if they have little to say, that lack is never discovered.

The Artist's Obituary

Artists should face the fact of their mortality in a pragmatic way. Since their families (if they have any) will have to deal with their funerals, someone will have to write their obituaries—and no one would like to get an obituary that reads something like "almost triumphed, but lacked talent." With the objective to prevent such a terrible obituary, artists who find themselves in mortal danger, due to age, sickness, or drugs, should spread a false rumor about their demise and work with a trusted friend to spread the news amongst a few AW personalities, working with a trusted friend to transmit the news. These people's immediate reactions should be meticulously recorded, as these will tend to be very candid. Once this process is completed, the artist will analyze the general tone of these comments and write an obituary designed counter such responses. The ready-to-go obituary should be entrusted to a lawyer and published as a disguised infomercial in *Artforum* and *The New York Times*. Self-made obituaries should be generous but may not use too many superlatives in order not to distort reality overly. In the case of artists without any hope of positive comments about their work after their death, a personality-based obituary will be written, saying things like "he was a wonderful person," or employ a variation of the classic obituary by a music critic about the famously untalented singer Florence Foster Jenkins: "her attitude was at all times the one of an artist that performed to the best of her abilities."

Back Door Operations

More often than not, an artist will not produce very memorable, or competent, art, and in many cases the work will not be very good at all. In these circumstances, artists can resort to certain strategies that may not entirely replace the lack of a true artistic talent, but which will certainly compensate and make a career out of very limited artistic abilities. Back

Door Operations are those activities in which artists engage in order to indirectly support their careers. These operations can include opening a gallery, starting a magazine or an art advertising company, or befriending important artists and becoming their de facto "handler" or informal dealer. The contacts and quid pro quos yielded by these strategies often result in attractive opportunities. Back door operations, however, cannot function as a permanent artist-support strategy.

If maintained for more than a year or two, the artist almost invariably (and unconsciously) ends up assuming the role of dealer, critic or whatever back-door identity he had originally created.

The Critic

Basic Principles

As we can see elsewhere in this manual, art critics are without a doubt a key element in the process of evaluating artistic production. Without them, every artwork would be considered exceptional and without any possibility of improvement. It is thus necessary to have a number of critical voices to blow the whistle on those artworks which have no merit whatsoever, as well as valuing those for which the public may not care. It is true that, in the artistic hierarchy, the critics are traditionally the most despised figures—and, paradoxically, the most sought after. It is argued that critics are formed from socially isolated youths—isolated by lack of popularity or other sad reasons. This isolation generates ideal conditions for observation as well as an innate ability to comment about what is being observed. Here we outline a few tenets that the critic must follow in order to best function in the AW:

1. The critic should show absolute neutrality in the social environment. It is important for the critic to know that, at the moment in which he or she enters a gallery, tensions will rise, and the dealer will obsessively scrutinize the critic's most minimal expressions and comments. It is important that the critic to maintain a stoic, "totem pole" expression.
2. The critic should keep a levelheaded attitude regarding his or her self-esteem. For good or for bad, the only reason he or she

will be invited to high-level social events and be given special treatment is because the power of his or her potential (and hopefully positive) critique. Thus a critic who abandons (or is fired from) his or her job and sees a sharp decline in high-level invitations may fall into a deep depression. It is recommended to all critics who leave their jobs to also leave the country, and if possible, leave the AW as far behind as possible.

3. Art critics should be particularly scrupulous in hiding the unsuccessful artistic career of their youths (every critic has one), which, without a doubt, if discovered, will be the focus of every criticism and humiliation from the AW.
4. Similarly, under no circumstances should the critic share his or her current artistic creations, in particular poetry, with the public (see previous point).
5. In their reviews, critics should appear to be democratic, even though it may be apparent in which artists, mediums and ideas they are interested and to which they are particularly opposed.

The Critic in the Public Forum

Critics are highly public figures who often speak at public events, round-table discussions, giving lectures and interviews in the media. Such distinction is bestowed in order to compensate the general, if unspoken, dislike of the AW toward their profession.

The critic at all times should adopt a serious expression while making public commentary. A lack of serious expression will result in a failure to transmit a sense of authority by the critic's comments. Critics are encouraged to make slight facial gestures, signaling boredom, knowledge of a certain subject, or disregard for the comments of another, while in panels and symposia. These gestures will allow them to better connect with the audience.

The Critic for Hire and the Commissioned Essays

Most of us know that critics can hardly survive with the minuscule payments they receive for their reviews in magazines and newspapers (payments which, by the way, tend to be delayed for up to six months and can only generally cover a medium-scale restaurant dinner at most). This is why they need to find other methods of survival. One is the essay for hire. In the case of artists that the critic admires, these kinds of jobs represent no challenge at all. However, the opposite case, that is, the critic is sought by artists with limited or questionable talent who desperately need his/her endorsement, tends to be the most frequent. In those cases, the critic (or the historian or the curator) faces an ethical dilemma, caught between making a living and gambling his or her reputation by writing on the work of this questionable artist (a negative essay would of course not be an option). As a result, this is one of the greatest challenges a critic can face, and one that most likely is faced by every critic eventually.

Following are a few guidelines to the writing process of such texts:

a) *Do not attempt to argue the impossible.* Some critics and curators will try to argue in their essays that the artist's work is indeed valuable—and some may even achieve a level of argument appearing as if they themselves were absolutely convinced of it. Some of them, the good writers, may manage to transmit their defense for the artist with enough passion, but such arguments may only end up in convincing the reader that the writer has fallen into a temporary critical lapse, and the common wisdom will conclude that the artist's work is bad regardless.
b) Upon beginning the essay, the writer should make a vague and generic philosophical reflection around the genre that the artist is working on. It is desirable to quote Benjamin and Sontag if writing about photography, Foucault and Derrida if about conceptual art, Adorno and Deleuze if the work addresses genre, and Greenberg and Danto if speaking about painting.
c) The writer should make a vague and generic reflection about the themes on which the artist is working, thus moving on toward a theoretical "simulacrum" around the topic. Such "simulacrum" can be made by confronting the theories of the previously mentioned writers, in any combination.
d) Immediately proceed to mention the manner in which the artist's work connects with these theories. It goes without saying that the connection one will establish will likely be a

bit arbitrary, given the likelihood that the artist either will not know about these theories or the work may not make any sort of significant contribution toward these ideas. Nevertheless, and depending on the talent of the essay's author, it is possible to build a bridge from the theoretical abstraction toward a generic description of the artists' work, helping to place the work in a relatively acceptable framework laid out by theorists.

e) The critic should, out of self-protection, keep him or herself away from any value judgment about the artist. Many writers have demonstrated that it is possible to simply establish the arbitrary references and elaborate on that point, thus protecting one's unsentimental credibility.

f) Under no circumstances should the author try to establish significant links between the work of this artist and others, either of the artist's generation or from previous periods, especially if the compared artists are of great stature. Such contextualization will only reveal the artist's limitations against the worth of the other's.

On Reviews

Reviews—that form of writing concomitantly feverishly desired and bitterly hated by the AW, are the critic's weapons. Everyone will pretend that they have not read them when they are negative, and all will say they read them if they are positive (everyone reads them, in either case). No one will be ever in total agreement with them, unless they are entirely positive and refer to oneself. The critic should thus be aware of the psychological and emotional impact of his or her reviews and the ability that these have to throw any artist into profound depression, or euphoria. For this reason, the critic should learn how to coldly calculate his or her reader's primary reactions—since, if they are overly negative, the critic's life may even be in danger.

1. The review should at least generate the impression that the critic was actually at the exhibition space. (Many critics write reviews after having merely passed the exhibition, and sometimes without even having physically been in the space—having checked the information from the internet.)

2. The review should begin from the premise that the critic did at least enter the space well disposed; otherwise the readership will conclude that the critic had already a judgment about the work before entering, which sometimes is the case.
3. The review should have "emotional rhythm." This means that a good reviewer should not announce his opinion on the work until nearly the last paragraph. This allows the review, like a classic Hollywood movie, to be enjoyed with great expectation both by those who are in favor of, and those who are against, the exhibition. If such effect is attained, the last phrase can have the power of a firework explosion if it is positive or the pain of a sharp knife cutting skin if it is negative.

Sentimental Unions in the AW

It is a fact that, sooner or later, sentimental relationships evolve in any professional environment. Given the inevitability of unions caused by love, the AW is generally disposed to accept practically any combination that may take place. Nevertheless, it is very important for art professionals to be aware of relationships in the greater context of their careers. While some relationships can initially be advantageous (for example, between curators and artists) after passing time they may become detrimental to the less prominent member of the couple (either the curator or the artist). As one may appreciate from the following chart, there are different levels of external "acceptability" in certain relationships, in the public perception of a certain relationship.

Chart of Sentimental Relationships

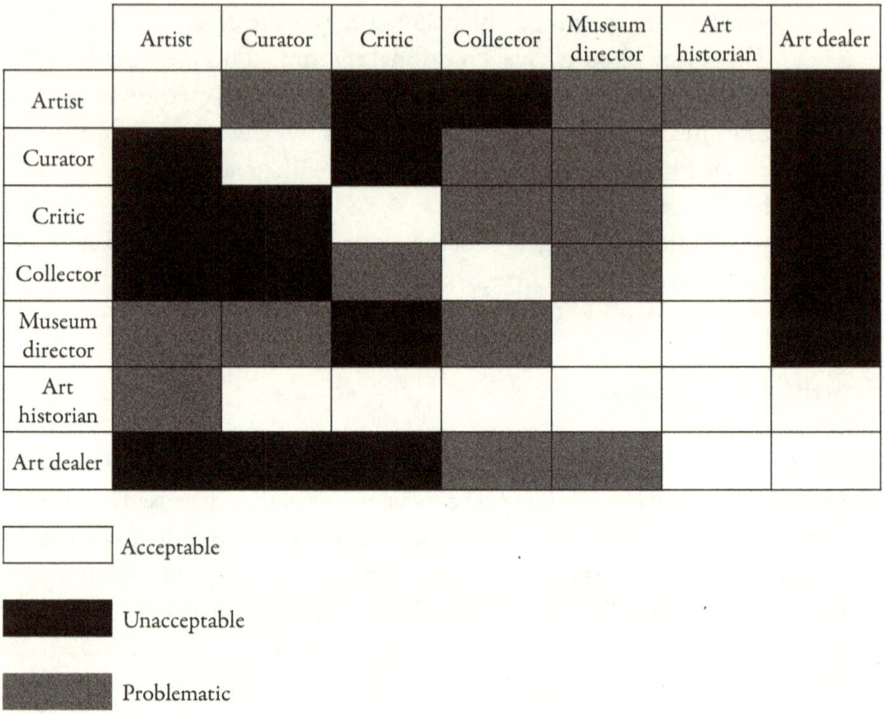

	Artist	Curator	Critic	Collector	Museum director	Art historian	Art dealer
Artist							
Curator							
Critic							
Collector							
Museum director							
Art historian							
Art dealer							

Acceptable

Unacceptable

Problematic

According to a general measure, the professionals of a same rank and category may join without conflict (although many caution against the union between two artists). Art historians are generally the ideal partners, since they are the least involved in economic or political aspects of the AW. Artists and art dealers, on the other hand, are the ones who create a more conflict-ridden relationship. To those it is recommended, if possible, to find a partner outside of the AW.

3. THE SOCIAL OCASSIONS

Ideal Social Choreography for an Artist at an Opening

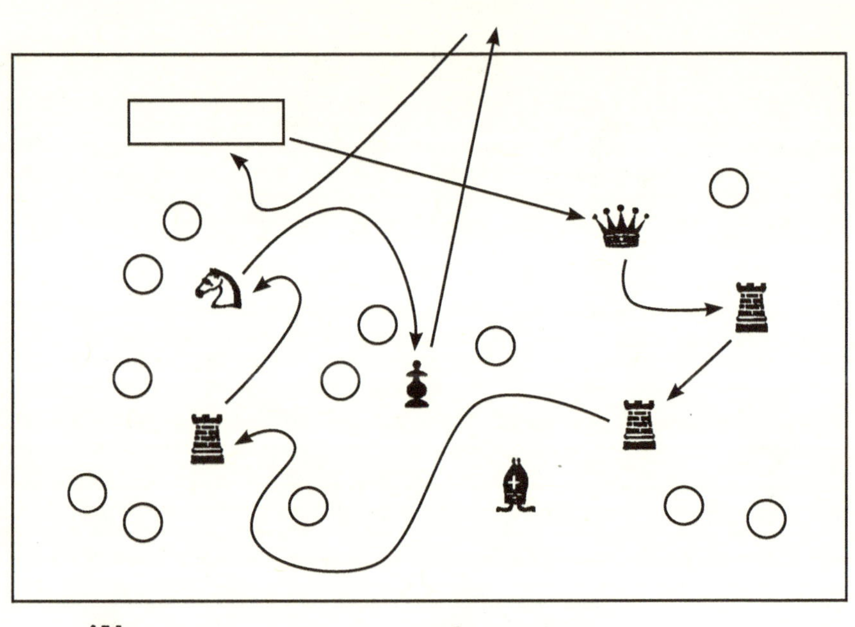

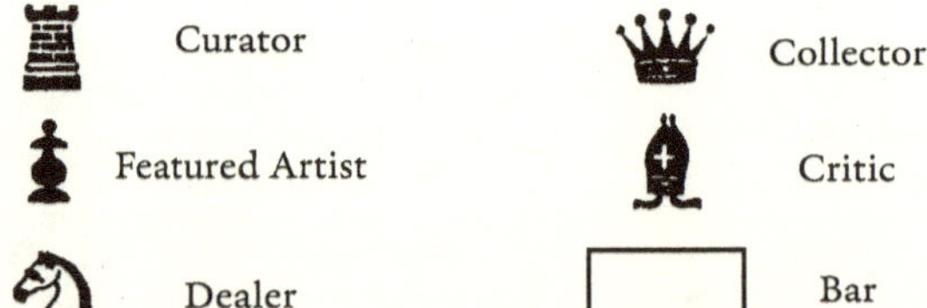

Openings

Openings, also known as *vernissages*, are crucial events where various interactions propel the dynamics of contemporary art life. In the tradition of nineteenth century balls, openings are comprised of a complex choreography of interested individuals or parties who weave around each other in a harmonious and sophisticated manner exchanging niceties, while at the same time finding opportunities to further their agendas or interests. Openings have a commercial subtext, since almost all of those in attendance have something to offer and to promote. The subtleties of social and financial interaction can profoundly confound the purposefully or accidentally naïve visitor who may come to an opening just to "see the art."

The experienced opening-reception visitor knows that each one of those in attendance has something to offer his or her career. As in the previously discussed game of chess, it is the professional's duty to reach the most important pieces of the game.

The ideal choreography for an artist at an opening can be seen in the facing diagram. It is important to note that, in terms of the actual career interests of the artist, the exhibiting artist is the least important person of the evening, but one has to make sure still to greet him or her. The artist visitor will have, as a primary objective, to arrive to the table with drinks and hors d'oeuvres. Once having drink and food at hand, one will need to survey the room, to determine who are the most important persons to approach. One has to operate in a hierarchical manner, starting with collectors and curators, and avoiding the critics (as mentioned before, the interaction between artists and critics is best when reduced to a minimum).

It is essential for the visitor to walk through the gallery and approach the event with absolute elegance and indifference; carefully displayed indifference can be an indicator of power.

In contrast, impulsively approaching people or being self-promotional immediately, are indicators of desperation to all, and, as a result, generate the impression that the artist cannot maneuver within the AW. Blatant self-promotion is considered in bad taste and generally associated with amateur artists. Even though it arises from a pragmatic attitude and goes directly to the objective of appearing at openings, nobody likes to see someone disregard the appearance of social refinement that these events have. There are several ways of tastefully inserting self-promotion into a conversation:

1. No artist or curator, during an opening, should initiate a conversation promoting his or her work. Before mentioning one's work, one must wait for someone in the group to ask about his or her job.
2. No artist should excessively show off his or her recent achievements or recognitions, especially in the presence of other artists who may find themselves in a much less advantageous position. Such an approach tends to depress and to cause envy in other artists.
3. While an artist is speaking about his or her achievements, one should never interrupt, and even less should one interject phrases implying competition, such as "I also was at that biennial." Such phrases will indicate that the other person is trying to minimize the importance of what the artist is narrating.
4. Party guests will flee from those who do nothing but self-promoting themselves. It is important in any conversation to ensure that giving the opportunity to others to speak, so that we may also get a chance to interject our own message.
5. The finest self-promotion is the one that takes place without making any explicit announcements, but instead influencing the interlocutor to cue us to speak about that in which we are interested. For example, international artists may like to exaggerate their jetlag, as this implies that they have a heavy travel schedule because they are in great demand. Using the subject of their tiredness and jetlag can be an elegant entry to proceed to talk about their work, as long as they are invited to do so. Conversations may proceed "I am so tired because I just arrived from Amsterdam" to which the response may be "Oh, and what where you doing in Amsterdam?"
6. It is important to remember that if we are not asked about our work (in whatever capacity we may work) most likely is not worth it to attempt to speak about it—lack of interest is an indication that we have the wrong audience for our purposes.

7. For those who carry exhibition postcards with them, they must be careful to distribute these in good taste and not like someone who distributes flyers to every passerby. One should ideally give out an exhibition postcard only when he or she is asked about the upcoming exhibition.
8. During group conversations at openings, it is a common tendency amongst artists and curators alike to take over the discussion, commencing with an endless recitation of all their projects. Such tendency is not only in bad taste, but is also counterproductive and suspicious. The reasoning is that, if one has so many projects and takes them all seriously, one would not spend time attending social events. Although this manual does not recommend that listeners point this out to the speaker, it is understood that some people may reply with phrases to the effect of "Wow, you are so busy, I am astounded that you have time for social occasions."
9. Dress code during openings depends, of course, on the kind of space that one is visiting and the kind of opening one is attending. Ideally, one should be familiar with the style of openings that the gallery organizes in order to make an informed decision. Some galleries encourage Hawaiian shirts, while others will disapprove of anything other than Prada (or a knockoff, if one does not have the financial resources for authentic). Only collectors are given complete freedom to dress as they may like; they are not under any pressure to impress anyone. There are, of course, those artists who like to dress and behave in an extravagant manner and will do so at every kind of opening and high-level social event. According to some of them, this is due not to their interest in drawing attention to themselves, but simply because they cannot conform their artistic personality to the fashion expectations of a formal occasion. Some of these artists may arrive with props—flowery hats, teddy bears, provocative and/or revealing clothing, spears or golden capes. It is not appropriate for the other visitors to criticize these fashion decisions or laugh at the artists because doing so would be as cruel as ridiculing their art in public. These artists are known as having *repressed creativity*, since they have had the bad luck of not having or finding enough ways of expressing themselves given the

lack of interest in their work. It is thus important to treat these artists with utmost respect. Hopefully, with collective acceptance they will manage to overcome their creative repression.

What to Say When We Don't Like the Work

Many believe that to "tell the truth" during the opening is the most important thing. Nevertheless it is considered in very poor taste to depress the artist on that night, since it is his or her work that is being celebrated. In those cases, it is recommended to make neutral comments about the appreciation of the work, such as "Congratulations," "I am impressed by the amount of work," "Great turnout," or "I have to come back to look at it carefully, but congratulations."

Length of Stay at an Opening

When there is a large crowd and one can escape without being noticed, it is enough to come right in and out, only saying hello to the key persons involved (see opening choreography diagram). However, if attending a semi-empty opening, it is not appropriate to stay for less than fifteen minutes. In case one is the only attendee at an opening after than the artist and the dealer, it is the duty of the attendee to remain in the gallery until at least another visitor arrives. If no one else arrives, the attendee must stay in the space until the artist deems that the event is over. Once this happens, it is good manners to invite to the artist to a bar to drown his or her sorrows.

Opening Demographics

Here is one of the greatest points of confusion. Are openings a fair sample of the general demographics of the AW? The answer is yes and no. Those who attend openings are generally those who have time to attend openings, but more significantly openings are normally composed by those for whom attending openings is an equal or greater interest than taking care of their other professional activities. Some artists and curators actually claim to best conceive their work while socializing—taking ideas from others, improvising works, etc. In contrast, the most sought-after artists and curators, who are very absorbed in their work, will rarely be able to attend an opening. In the large AW cities, there are those who make opening attendance their full-time jobs. As a result, they are not able to do any activity other than relaying their conversations and experiences from previous openings.

Approaching Strangers at an Opening

Upon entering the exhibition space, the opening expert will know how to construct in the mind a quick topographical assessment of the room, mentally making creating a hierarchy of who are the most useful persons in attendance and with whom he or she needs to interact. As a general rule, it is important to start with the higher-level people who are currently available to talk. Opening attendees are evaluated in terms of "networking worth." But, what happens when it is essential for us to approach a person of great importance whom we have not actually met? Following are a few etiquette rules to solve this little problem gracefully.

To approach important people (magazine editors, influential artists, collectors, international curators, etc.) without having someone to introduce us can be an extremely difficult task, and is not recommended unless one possesses experience and social refinement.

The person to be approached (the "aproachee") will likely have experience with being regularly approached by people who have not had the opportunity to read this manual and may likely try to engage them in a rather annoying way—forcing the important person to listen through long proposals, advertisements, offers, and interminable, pointless comments about any given topic. It is important to realize that the important person will likely initiate any conversation with caution, and may show certain impatience to those who, in the very first seconds of the interaction, employ the aforementioned verbal patterns.

1. The expert "approacher," as a general rule, should be knowledgeable of the biography and work of those he or she decides to approach. This generally allows the famous person to become more receptive.
2. In order to open the conversation, it always helps to mention a person that both may share in common. If this is the case you may say something like "I believe you know X, who is someone of which I am also very fond."

3. The approacher should have prepared a conversation plan for this person, preferably one that may not last longer than a minute. If one does not have a clear idea why he or she is approaching this person, and the dialogue turns only around small talk, it is recommended to cut short the conversation.
4. The approacher should always try to keep a sincerely interested and serene expression. Any kind of excessive emotional expression may be seen as amateurish.
5. It is important not to show excessive awe in front of an important curator, collector, or artist. In the case of the unexpected appearance of a famous person during a social event, everyone should try to appear indifferent, since any sort of expression of nervousness, excitement or expression of the desire to get someone's autograph (unless if it is for an art project) will immediately indicate the person's inability to handle these situations, and will reveal that he or she is not capable of conducting him or herself on the level of these people.
6. Once the first step is taken to approach someone, it is entirely up to the generosity and humanity of that renowned person to allow one to establish a conversation. We did a brief study at a number of openings, disguising our researchers as aspiring artists without any "networking worth" whatsoever, and making them approach well known AW professionals. On the scale of 1 to 10, we tabulated the approachability of each person, 10 being the highest level of approachability, 6 as median, and 0 being completely unapproachable, turning his or her back to the artist in the middle of the phrase to speak to someone of greater relevance.

Arthur Danto	10
Gilbert and George	9.9
Yuko Hasegawa	9.5
Hans Ulrich-Obrist	9.2
Glen Lowry	9
Matthew Barney	8.6
Dan Cameron	8.4
Stan Douglas	8
Thelma Golden	7.9
Francesco Bonami	5.7
Rosalind Krauss	5.2
Klaus Biesenbach	4.8
Jim Dine	3.4
Rachel Whiteread	2.3
Richard Serra	1
Thomas McEvilley	0

It is important to note that this behavioral study at openings, while it cannot be deemed entirely scientific, has incited debates that it is the more successful people, and generally the ones with greatest talent, who are the most generous in conversations, and that the intelligence and education of the subjects is inversely proportional to their openness to speak to people whose conversation may not offer an immediate benefit whatsoever.

At the beginning of a conversation, it is bad form to subject anyone to listening to an artist's self-promotion. Self-promotion, like erotic seduction, must begin with subtlety. The artist will have to approach the interlocutor with grace and gentleness, and without making it seem that the primary interest is to self-promote. If the artist is successful, he or she will be awarded the opportunity to discuss his or her work. If this does not happen, it indicates that the interlocutor is definitely not interested in learning about the artist's work and the conversation should be left at that.

Flattery Etiquette

It is generally believed that flattery is the easiest part of a conversation, as well as the most direct way to establish and maintain a good relationship with an art professional. In the AW, nevertheless, to flatter a person can be extremely difficult (even without including the instances in which a person has difficult traits that may be worth praising). Excessive flattery is usually detected as fake and is looked upon as vulgar. Important people in the AW are used to receiving excessive flattery constantly, and while they will thank the flatterer, they will likely think less of him or her. Nevertheless, no one, famous or not, is immune to flattery. On the contrary, we all want to hear a creative flattering comment about ourselves. The expert flatterer will have the ability to seduce his or her subject in such a way that, as a result of his or her comments, he or she will develop a sound relationship with this person. The appropriate etiquette for flattery is as follows:

1. Avoid any sort of commonplace flattering comments, such as "you are the artist who has influenced me most." Do not make any overly intimate comments, such as "I have a poster of your work next to my bed." Such phrase could generate apprehension and even fear in the person addressed.
2. If one is to flatter an artist, one has to study the artist's work in depth and make reference not to his or her most important or famous work, but rather one of the least known or critically least-favored works. This will please the artist very much. Similarly, when dealing with a curator or critic, it is useful to praise a book or essay that has been particularly criticized. The curator or critic will then feel that they finally have found someone who understands the complexity of that work.
3. One must try to bury the praise within a certain phrase, instead of making it the centerpiece of the comment. To say something like "you are the best artist of your generation" will only make the artist blush without knowing what to say. Instead, one can say something to the effect of "how do you usually handle the jealousy that all the artists of your generation must certainly have toward you?" which will give several opportunities to

the artist to reply with humor and elegance while flattering him or her.

4. The flatterer must give himself/herself very little importance at the moment of making the praise. Professional flatterers tend to announce their praising comments as if they were giving out a prize. This only creates an embarrassing situation for everyone. Instead, praise that is brought into the conversation with humility and discretion is very well received.

How to Make Innuendos

There are situations in which one suffers the unacceptable behavior of a certain person and thus is compelled to say something about it. Even in the cases of greatest provocation, it is unacceptable to descend to the level of this person, but there are a number of elegant ways through which we can express our dissatisfaction with this person's deportment:

1. In the case of someone who is showing off a certain award or distinction, and endlessly holds the conversation hostage by reciting a list of commendations, it is correct to interject by saying "you are so lucky!" This insulting phrase delicately suggests that it is mere chance, and not the talent of the person that enabled him or her to receive this distinction.
2. If a person is dedicated to negatively criticizing every kind of work and generally shows a destructive disposition toward everything that he or she views, it is recommended to agree with this person and to be even more destructive with every single comment. Once this person is confronted with the maximum extreme of destructive critique, he or she will feel obligated to acknowledge that he or she must to tone down his or her criticisms.
3. If an art professional shows a constant competitive behavior, interrupting people with phrases that exaggerate his or her importance, knowledge or accomplishment, it is correct for the group to completely ignore this person, as if his or her conversation were not even heard.
4. Sometimes a person will claim to have been to a certain exhibition or to have seen a certain art event, just for the sake of

continuing to have a role in a conversation, while we will know that this person was not in attendance. It will be correct to thoroughly quiz the person about the minutest details of the event until the person retracts his or her statements or feels forced to change the subject.

On Business Cards

Business cards are of singular importance in the AW. Since they are the first indicator of who we are, it is important to know how to design them with great style and elegance and how to offer them to the people around us.

In design, business cards may vary greatly depending on the personality of their owner. They should be neither too original nor too flashy. One should consider the following guidelines:

1. It is bad taste to give out inkjet-printed business cards, which will be evident due to their indented borders.
2. On the business card, one should not include a picture of oneself, much less in a provocative pose.
3. In the text, do not use any kind of superlatives to describe oneself.
4. In selecting fonts, it is not recommend using the fonts Sans Comic, Curlz, or Dingbats, unless one may be a children's art educator.

During social events, such as openings, the following rules apply to handing out business cards:

1. One should never extend one's card to another person without having engaged in a conversation.
2. One should never make evident that one has the business card handy; such readiness will indicate that promoting oneself is the sole objective of the interaction.
3. Never offer a card to someone who has food and drink in his or her hands and never try to insert a card into a shirt pocket or in the cleavage of a dress.

4. It is bad etiquette, when in a group, to give out a card to a single person, especially when this person is evidently more important than the others in the group (for instance, if this person is a curator within a group of artists). The correct action is to offer a card to the members of the whole group.

How to Visit an Exhibition Space

Many individuals, whether professionals or novices, experience a certain uneasiness upon entering an exhibition space showing contemporary art. This uneasiness is perfectly understandable, since exhibition spaces are usually not designed to put the viewer at ease but rather to transmit class and credibility (particularly in the case of galleries). Most of us, when entering an exhibition space, may ask ourselves things like: "am I sufficiently sophisticated to come into this place?" "What might happen if I do not behave well enough?" "Might I be intimidated by the complexity of the work that I'll encounter?"

In this section we will analyze the duties of the exhibition visitor and the minimally adequate behavior one must observe during such a visit.

1. Visitors should enter slowly and with grace into the exhibition space. This rule cannot be applied if the space is too crowded, in which case one should enter in whatever manner possible. The visitor's manner of dress should preferably mimic a collector's fashion (a dark suit can do the trick) in order to be treated with most respect. Women should not wear excessive jewelry or large hairpieces that may compete with the artworks. It is also bad form to wear too much perfume at crowded exhibition openings. Since a lot of people will gather around several works, it is inevitable that the perfume will impregnate their respective clothes, lingering well after they return home. It is considered bad manners when performance artists enter crowded exhibitions smeared in stinking smells in order to clear space around them in order to see the works.
2. The educated visitor should not show any surprise, anger, or enthusiasm while regarding the exhibition. It is best to adopt a calm, reserved and serene attitude at all times. On occasion,

it is acceptable to nod the head, as if the work has been recognized.

3. The visitor should make every effort to see the exhibition in its entirety. There is always the possibility that the last work in the last corner of the gallery may have been overlooked. This may cause an embarrassing problem if this one work belongs to an artist that one knows or may meet. If the visitor claims to have seen the exhibition but does nor recall that one work, it could be highly offensive to the artist.
4. The visitor is expected to see a painting or photograph for an average of one and a half minutes. Videos must be watched from beginning to end, no matter their length.
5. Visitors should be prepared to defend their comments regarding the exhibition. Nowadays, more and more visitor services departments are implementing a policy of "visitor interpretive responsibilities." For example, in some museums, if one is on a museum tour and says something like "my four year old son could have made this work," the museum authorities can rightfully demand this visitor to first, produce the four-year old son in the gallery and then, prove that the boy indeed is capable of reproducing the exact work as mentioned, being given the adequate materials. Those visitors who may say that a work "is not art" will be invited by the security staff into the museum's offices and will be asked to remain there until he or she produces a 4000-word essay on why the aforementioned work is not art, offering the adequate historical contexts, authoritative references and complete bibliography. While we believe that these requirements may become excessive, it is in the interest of the museum visitor to be prepared for such interpretive eventualities.
6. In galleries, it is *de rigueur* to sign the visitor's book. The book establishes a "who's who" of the visitors. It is in bad taste to sign with a fictional name, or to tear and take the sheet containing the signature of any given celebrity.

Q&A

Sometimes, while visiting a gallery or a museum, one may be entertained to the point of laughter. Is it bad to laugh at an exhibition space?

It is indeed bad to laugh at an exhibition. Both the artist and the exhibition staff may think that the laughter is not motivated by the pleasure derived from seeing the work but rather by mockery of it. Any excessive noise may also be considered a typical feature of an insecure visitor who only wants to draw attention.

Certain exhibitions have many lengthy video installations that would take the whole day to watch in their entirety. What should one do in those situations?

Lengthy video installations certainly pose a dilemma to the AW. Artists tend to exacerbate the problem by creating extremely long video works in spaces that smell like sweat, fresh paint and synthetic carpeting, and are uncomfortable, generally without any seating, etc. In these inconsiderate situations one must show discretion escaping from the video installation without being noticed. If this is not possible, and one is inside the space with other visitors, one should leave making a casual comment like "I saw the rest earlier . . . it's a great work. You need watch the entire video to fully appreciate it."

Is it good manners to buy the catalogue upon leaving the exhibition? And, should one read the full catalogue after seeing the exhibition?

If one wants to give a good impression in the AW, one has to spend money. Buying the catalogue is a minimal gesture that serves this purpose. However, no one is expected to read the catalogue—including the organizers of the exhibition—given the fact that so many catalogues are produced that it would be impossible for anyone to read every one of them.

The Studio Visit

The studio visit is a professional ritual in which artists invite curators, critics, other artists, and even the public, to see their working environments. The studio visit's purpose is to promote the work of the artist. Understanding that curators are the most frequent studio visitors, here are some recommendations made with them in mind, although these guidelines may be beneficial for anyone who visits an artist studio.

1. The visitor should be aware that the studio visit can be a highly stressful occasion for the artist, especially if the visitor is in a position of power. The visitor should try not to worsen the situation by making comments in bad taste, such as referring to the small size of the studio, or mentioning the dangerous neighborhood where it is located.
2. Artists ideally expect results from the studio visit, whether it may be inclusion in an exhibition, the sale of a work, etc. The visitor should not make any gestures that inspire false hopes, such as showing too much enthusiasm. A neutral attitude is recommended, particularly toward departure, which is the defining point of a studio visit (and the time when an invitation, possible purchase, or something of the sort is mentioned). In general, it is appropriate to say a few words that express interest in the work but also express the visitor's need to assimilate what was seen during the visit.
3. It is in extremely bad taste to compare the work on view with that of a better known, and more accomplished, artist who may be working on the same subject. Such comparisons tend to depress the lesser-known artist.
4. The studio visit can become very challenging especially if the work of the artist is lacking in every respect. Even in these cases, it is the duty of the visitor to make intelligent and positive comments in regard to the work. Some useful comments that can be employed are:

- How long have you been working on these pieces?
- I notice that you have changed a lot from what you were doing before.
- I find your way of working with the material interesting.
- What is your favorite work in this group?
- What do you think your next series will concern?

4. PUBLIC RELATIONS ETIQUETTE

PR is the basis of any artwork, and even more so in the twenty-first century. The main problem for an artist in the AW is not only to make an interesting artwork but also to know how to promote it with adequate strategy and taste.

While money is necessary, the adequate marketing of a work or an artist is not something that can always be solved with a big budget. Strategy and promotional etiquette are essential in order to give a favorable impression of the work, the exhibition, the artist or whatever art product one may need to market.

The rules of adequate, sensible and effective PR are:

1. Effective promotion is achieved by a combination of direct and "oblique" promotion. "Oblique promotion" is a type of indirect PR that comes—or at least appears to come—from a third party. While a paid advertisement in a magazine has a certain impact, a critical article that magnifies the importance of the product and appears in the same publication provides a good balance of direct and "oblique" PR. Art magazines are very well aware of the power of oblique PR and, although they may not publish favorable reviews in exchange for advertising, a big advertiser should rightfully expect a better critical attention and perks from a magazine (favorable calendar plug-ins, slightly friendlier reviewers assigned to their shows, etc.). Oblique promotion, when it is well placed, can be highly effective.
2. The best kind of PR is the one not acknowledged as such. There is always the risk of over-promoting a product, tiring the public to the point and rendering the publicity counterproductive. It is recommended to employ strategies such as product insertion, oblique PR and third-party contracting. The successful promotion of a product is accomplished when one communicates the belief that life without the product is inconceivable.
3. The best PR strategy is to make the potential buyer believe he or she has discovered the value of the product independently.

This is known as "Hansel and Gretel Strategy." The artist, gallery or any other promoter will ideally generate a breadcrumb path for the buyer toward the product. The Hansel and Gretel strategy is employed when the dealer appears to have an almost indifferent attitude toward the works on display, as if they were not valuable at all.

4. As in any other business, word of mouth is the most effective promotional tool available—but at the same time is extremely hard to create artificially. There have been certain efforts by some artists to create artificial "buzz" about themselves by hiring actors to roam around art fairs and galleries speaking highly of their work. This strategy, while sometimes effective, may backfire if the scheme is discovered by others.

Writing Press Releases

One of the greatest challenges in PR is writing a good press release for an exhibition. Even though few people read press releases carefully, they are vital to announcing a product effectively. Press release language must be extremely careful and terse. Following are a few format rules for a gallery exhibition press release:

1. *First paragraph*. One starts with the phrase "The gallery X proudly presents the new exhibition of Z (artist name), entitled Y (exhibition title). Date, time and address should be included.
2. *Second paragraph*. This usually is the hardest section of the text, since it is here that the description of the artist and the work must be made. Nevertheless, as one will see in the useful combination chart below, there are only a certain number of variables that one can use to describe every possible project. It will suffice to choose any of the most appropriate selections as one builds each phrase.

A	B	C	D
His/her work	reflects upon	Modernism	in innovative ways.
	explores	its own genre	
	critiques	society	
	problematizes	personal experiences	
		conceptualism	

One can write "his work explores his personal experiences in innovative ways" or "his work critiques Modernism in innovative ways." Since we are dealing with contemporary art, every exhibition should be described as innovative.

3. *Third paragraph.* Here is where the works in the exhibition need to be described:

   "In the work ____, Z presents _____ (describe one of the works in the exhibition). In this work, one can appreciate ______ (describe what we want the viewer to appreciate in the work)."

   "In the work _____ (describe another work in the show), also included in the exhibition, the artist presents to us ______ (describe what is seen in this work), generating a reflection around (choose the word from the column "c" from the second paragraph)."

   "Z is a internationally recognized artist who has exhibited his work in many galleries and museums such as (in case that Z may not have exhibited in galleries or museums, the first part of the phrase can be still used, only eliminating the phrase "such as")."

   In the case of works without a great deal of content, it is recommended to use the strategy known as "hermetic communiqué." Hermetic communiqués are written using many adjectives, adverbs used as verbs, and prepositional phrases next to verbs that take the place of the subject. An example is:

"the exploration of intense interactivity of post-minimalism is interrogated in this re-construction of post-modern theoretical schemes." Given the fact that most readers will hardly have the time to sit to decode each phrase of the press release, the reading of this document will become something like an act of faith.

Self-Promotional Etiquette

1. The art of self-promotion is as old as art-making itself. Historically, self-promotion was practiced with subtle, and perhaps a bit naïve, methods. Throughout the twentieth century, thanks to the emergence of important self-promoters such as Picasso, Duchamp, Dali and later Beuys and Warhol, self-promotion, no longer perceived as taboo, and could be freely practiced by any artist. And yet, with the exception of certain B-level artists who have made their self-promotional efforts the actual artwork, self-promotion should be done delicately and with style. The professional artist will generally be the one who least gives the impression of actively promoting oneself.
2. Understandably, artists are always hungry for attention, but it is in their interest not to show their desire to be in the limelight (for this very reason, the strategy of the hermit-artist can be one of the most effective, since the artist who hides from the public creates an aura of mystery which generates fascination and interest from the public).
3. In their self-promotional endeavors, artists will have to show impeccable e-mail etiquette. It is well known that e-mail is currently the most effective way of promoting an artist or an exhibition. However, it is considered highly inelegant for an artist to spam people with announcements of his or her own exhibitions—this task should be done by the artist representative when possible, such as the gallerist, or perhaps a friend. Some artists invent a pseudonym or fictional assistant who may send e-mails on his or her behalf. Others have refined their art of self-promotion to the extent of generating sophisticated information businesses publicizing art via e-mail with the exclusive purpose of self-promotion as well as promoting

the exhibitions of those individuals and institutions who may eventually help them in their careers. The method works, although the artist may have to be careful not to include him or herself too often in the information system, so not to imperil the perception of the "impartial" nature of the service.

4. It is bad etiquette for an artist to copy an entire e-mail list without blind-copying the recipients. Without blind-copying, others may "steal" the addresses in order to send out their own invitations. As a result, one can end up receiving hundreds of unknown e-mails about exhibitions of questionable quality. Although this manual does not approve, some consider it appropriate to retaliate by sending viruses *en masse* to the spammer. A popular virus is teddybear.exe, which will immediately self-install, erase the spammer's hard disk and address book, and hijack his or her browser to redirect it to porn sites.
5. Some also recommend sending the virus teddybear.exe to any artists or galleries who may send unsolicited promotional e-mails with images larger than 3MB.
6. A useful promotional strategy is to speak in the third person. The strategy is known as "Caesar," for the famous emperor who invented it. It is a method that promotes instant "historization" by creating the perception that an objective voice is speaking about the artist. The strategy fails only due to the literary limitations of the author. This failing becomes apparent when the text includes such trite phrases as "is considered the best in the world," "without a doubt the most influential," etc.
7. If an artist is in the process of gaining fame, and particularly if he or she lives in a small artistic community in certain cities, he or she will usually be interviewed to give an opinion about all sorts of subjects. It is essential that the artist neither state publicly any real political opinions nor speak publicly about specific people from the AW. These actions could potentially generate retaliation from institutions or collectors.
8. Artists should not give written opinions. This is best, first, given the fact that visual artists are not eloquent writers in general, and, second, because written statements are hard to contradict once printed, and could, once again, offend people in a position to help the artist's career at some point.

9. If the artist must become involved in political subjects, it is important for them to limit their work and commentary to only those parameters that are pre-established and acceptable within the AW. For example, artists can freely criticize the government and the abstract processes of the war and the dehumanization of modernity, but it is completely unacceptable for them to make comments about or references to specific politicians, corporations, businesspeople or collectors, given that in the majority of cases these are the sources of funds to the institutions where artists present their works. Collectors in particular must remain untouchable at all times.

CV Etiquette

The CV (also known as "bio" "resume" or "curriculum") is essential to highlighting the experience of the artist.

1. If one has limited professional experience, it will be necessary to "inflate" the CV. Utterly false information in a CV is usually unsuccessful, aside from being unethical. However, euphemisms and embellished information can go a long way. For example, if one participated at an open exhibition, (i.e., where there was no curatorial selection process) one can conveniently omit that detail without necessarily lying about the nature of the event.
2. Do not elaborate a CV with more than 45 pages. Many artists attempt to equate quantity with quality by including childhood exhibitions, restaurant displays, etc.
3. More importantly than being the truthful reflection of an artist's experience, the CV can conceal, and even improve upon, any deficiency in the artist's curriculum. The level of ambiguity in the text will be directly proportional to the artist's experience. Anyone can use a phrase such as "X is an artist of great renown whose work as been nationally and internationally recognized, and has participated in many projects at the individual and collective level."
4. Do not include date of birth unless younger than 30. Do not include city or country of birth unless it is perceived as exotic.

Social Troubleshooting:
The Case of "Cabin Fever"

Although the AW should function in according to good manners, respect, and professionalism, there are circumstances in which certain social conditions in a professional environment deteriorate beyond improvement. A common one is known as "cabin fever," a syndrome that takes place in cities with a small artistic community, or in cities so large that they break down into neighborhood-based artist communities. In these situations, the members of that community will inevitably have to interact with a frequency that will go beyond any healthy levels, and as we know, familiarity breeds contempt. Seeing the same people day after day at the same exhibition openings results in strange behavior among members of that community. Some aspects that are common to this syndrome are:

1. *Cell formation*. Given the hierarchical homogenization that distinguishes a small social milieu, new subgroups tend to form, alienating those who are excluded and giving a sense of empowerment to those who are included.
2. *Polarized information*. In these communities, certain kinds of information circulate with great speed—such as personal gossip and rumors. But other kinds of information are hidden—particularly in respect to professional opportunities, the arrival of an influential curator, and the sharing of important contacts in the AW.
3. *Partialization of the global view*. Due to the intense dynamic that results from the isolation in these communities, the imagined artificial hierarchies start to influence the members of the group, making them really believe that the AW turns around them, and not the other way around.

Following are a few etiquette rules to overcome "cabin fever":

1. While attending social events, never share any information that may be too personal or intimate. Such information, as innocent as it may appear, can always be used against one.
2. Always claim that one does not belong to any particular group. To announce any sort of affiliation will inevitably invite the rejection of those excluded from that group.
3. It is important to remember that any negative comment one may make of anyone in these environments will inevitably reach that person anywhere between 24 and 48 hours.
4. One should limit physical presence at social events in these environments, so to minimize familiarity and to avoid partaking in local disputes.

5. SUCCESS AND FAILURE

Success and failure are realities of professional life in every field, and the AW is no exception to the rule. However, given the ups and downs that distinguish the AW from the business world, success and failure can be particularly dramatic. Both situations can actually be equally problematic for different reasons.

How to Survive the Lack of Recognition

Public acknowledgement is the measuring stick of every artist. It is manifested in different ways, usually many at the same time: invitations to biennials and museum shows, international magazine reviews, acquisition by important collections and so on. Sadly, few artists are sufficiently recognized. The great majority will not make it to the art history books, but will rather fall onto the category that we prefer to describe here as "under-recognized artists." To belong to this category is the source of great angst and depression. However, those who manage to assimilate this status are able to live it with dignity and, in some cases, to even ascend eventually to the "recognized artist" category. One may succeed in this if one follows the rules we outline here:

1. One should never call oneself "under-recognized." Artists should, until their last minute of their lives, project infinite self-assuredness. It is desirable for them to always look busy and, when seen in public, to have an ever-ringing cell phone (it is easy to contract a calling service for this purpose). Artists who find themselves neglected must adopt the tag of "emerging artist," which can be adopted until one is 45 years old. After that age, one should simply say that he or she aspires to keep a "low profile."
2. The under-recognized artist can compensate his or her lack of recognition in the AW, and the extra work time due to lack of projects and direct it toward self-promotion. Untalented artists may accomplish much simply by dedicating efforts and discipline to their PR activities. In many cases they can

accomplish much more than talented artists who are too disorganized or busy to exploit their talents.

The "Selling Artist" Problem

This category is worth discussing given that is generates constant confusion in the AW. The AW is comprised of many sub-markets that live off the main market (derivative market, decorative market, secondary market, etc.) B, C, or even D-level artists who do not enter the true international market, or those who originally enter it but fall out of favor, go on to take part in the sub-markets that either sustain them financially or preserve their reputations locally. This can create confusion, when one sees an artist who is financially successful but whose work is not of particular relevance to the international AW. "Selling artists," by selling their work to a relatively reduced group of buyers, generate the impression that their work is indeed in great demand. These artists project the appearance that they are highly important but they continue to hold great resentments toward the AW for the rejection they feel. When interacting with them, one should make sure to never point out their deficiencies.

The Problem of the Successful Artist

It may come as a surprise to many people to refer to success as a problem. Not only is success a highly dangerous position in which to be, but it also tends to be a much more complicated problem than failure. Many artists survive failure, either by returning to their everyday lives or changing professions, but there are very few artists who survive success.

We need to start by defining what a successful artist is. Some artists consider themselves successful when their work is selling (look at "selling artist" section). Others, while successful in regards to their historical contribution, fail financially. And others, who have failed both financially and historically, may still believe themselves successful, and their belief may be so powerful that it proves contagious with the public, making the artists, effectively, into successful artists.

Success may arrive overnight, sometimes by mistake, but always in an unexpected manner. It can come by having created an anti-religious or sexually provocative work that suddenly triggers a controversy. Other times success comes slowly, and sometimes so slowly that it is posthumous. In any case, the living artist can be prepared to face the eventualities of success by following these rules:

1. Success results often in product homogenization. Artists should be prepared for endless requests to make additional versions of their most famous works. These requests will be difficult to refuse, since they will come from influential institutions and individuals, and there will be a lot of money involved. Artists should prepare for this by taking courses on quality control in industrial production. Otherwise, not being able to handle the demand that will arise on the work, success will not last for long.
2. Success originates the *international artist* syndrome, also known as the *festivalist* syndrome. The artist will be thrown into a situation in which he or she is hardly ever able to return to the studio, and spends most of the time traveling around the world, in airports and three-star hotels. The artist's work will have to adapt its subject to its own traveling experience in order to assimilate the artist's international routine. It is recommended to take an urban anthropology class, in order to avoid the creation of certain commonplace images amongst international artists, such as photographs of a street market in Manila.
3. Successful artists, as mentioned in the first section of this manual, are like the pawn that arrives to the eighth square. The artist's career will have to shift art-making to a secondary position and rather focus on politics. Thus it is no longer artistic talent, bur rather his or her sagacity as a politician that will guarantee the artist a high position.

Rejection in Art

Nothing is tougher than finding oneself in the position of rejecting someone. As it is the case with romantic love, the rejection of another's advances, whether it is to see someone's work, the invitation to participate at an exhibition, or writing about the work, is an extremely delicate task that requires the absolute consideration of the rejected person's feelings.

1. *The curatorial negative.* The most difficult task for a curator, apart from getting money for an exhibition, is to reject an artist. Highly susceptible artists take the slightest sign of rejection as an order demolishing their self-esteem. In these cases, the curator must convince the artist that, rather than his or her work being inferior to the planned exhibition, the case is the opposite.
2. *Declining to participate in exhibitions.* In the case of those artists invited to participate in a show that is not of interest, they should never give out the real reason for the decision to decline (such as the gallery's low quality, bad theme, low curatorial level, bad artists in the show, etc.). In general, it is much better to express great enthusiasm for the invitation, but answering that it is impossible to participate at this time because of too many previous engagements or not enough available work.
3. *Lecture invitations.* Both artists and curators may find themselves at some time in their careers having committed to too many engagements, or double and triple bookings, in which case one or more events must be canceled in order to give priority to the more important one. It is important not to tell the truth while canceling, but to devise an excuse such as sickness. We suggest, however, not to create excuses that are too obviously fictional (such as a broken hip or back fracture) if one is not 100% sure that he or she will not run into the people on which one has cancelled.
4. *Romantic/sexual rejection.* Those curators and other individuals in positions of power who are rejected by someone in a lesser position, are urged not to try to exterminate the career (or in some extreme cases, the life) of the person, since these attempts will likely backfire in the professional sense.

Controversy Etiquette

No topic is hotter than controversial art, given that it is the one kind of art that can grab both the media and the public's attention. This is why controversy is constantly sought after by artists, and sometimes, by institutions. However, controversy is a double-edged sword that must be handled with care.

1. Controversy has its acceptable limits. The AW promotes the liberty of the artist to do as he or she wishes, as long as they do not stray too far from the following rules: a) The artist can make direct attacks on the system, but is not allowed to use first names, unless these belong to people unknown in the AW. b) the artist should never attack, under any circumstance, any collector. The artist should never ridicule them, insult their intelligence or lack thereof, question their knowledge of art history, comment on their private life or sexual preferences or make any mention of their financial dealings inside and/or outside the AW. c) Controversial art does not require any sort of moral logic. However, one must remember that the artist is making contemporary art, which is grounded in a series of more or less liberal philosophical ideas about culture. Given this fact, the produced art must have some sort of liberal logic, even if this logic leads the artist to exploit others. As long as there is an explanation of what this art denounces, it will be regarded as artistically sound (unless, again, it attacks collectors in any way).
2. Controversy must be entertaining. Many artists consider as controversial acts pomposity or simply aggression. Actually, controversy is an art which, although it can humiliate others, does so with great elegance. Artists should be careful to commit their controversial acts with great care and sometimes with complicity with the public so that it feels included.
3. In order to make good controversial art, one must find simple ideas and show them in an accessible way. Controversial art in general is not a lofty kind of art, but the benefits are the

same as those for the real artist. Just as success is unexpected, that which is controversial happens in an unexpected manner. Those who designate a work as controversial by denouncing it tend to be people with no relation to the AW—such as religious leaders or politicians. Given the fact that these become the "selectors" of the controversial work, the artist who seeks controversy should make sure that the offensive ideas and symbols are fairly easy for the layperson to comprehend.

4. Adequate topics for controversy are: sex, religion, and conservative values.

Art-making Under a Dictatorship

Art making can be a life or death activity, as many artists who live under dictatorships have proved. And yet, living under political hardship provides an excellent opportunity for an artist to create work with a strong subject matter which will generally be viewed sympathetically by the AW.

Most artists working under dictatorships make metaphorical art. The artist's imagination will be focused on producing works incomprehensible to the dictatorial government, but readable in the external market.

Biting the Hand of the Feeder

One may ask: if someone has a foundation grant or the support of a museum to produce a work of art, is it appropriate to criticize them? Foundations, organizations and museums are usually very enthusiastic to have the artist offer an institutional critique, as this will make them appear transparent. However, the artist should observe the rules established before (i.e., do not mention the institutions' trustees).

A Final Question

If an artist makes a work consisting of making a loaded gun available to the public and inviting them to shoot the artist, and if someone actually accepts the challenge, is it appropriate to end the performance or would it be bad etiquette to do so?

At the onset of conceptualism, it would have considered bad etiquette to do so. According to early logic, it was better to die than to compromise the work. However, as each aspect of the AW is compromised and regulated, such extremity makes little sense, nor does it make sense to actually perish for the supposed integrity of art. As one will have seen in this manual, the AW etiquette operates on the premise of living off art, not dying for art. The viewer would need to be aware that, while the artist is being offered to be shot, he is not serious. After all, it is just art. It would be unfortunate for the viewer to have to intervene and kill the one naïve audience member, but if one has integrity and if one has observed the flawless behavioral guidelines established by this manual, it will be highly satisfactory for him or her to know that one has followed the most impeccable etiquette by so doing.

GLOSSARY

Academy
The word is understood as encompassing any form of art that has become, over the years, mechanized to the point of being a creative system able to be learned practically anywhere, by anybody, and taught by anyone. Today's academy promotes global conceptualism and relational aesthetics.

Adornamentation
Term that emerges from the fusion of the term "ornamentation" and the name of the philosopher Theodor W. Adorno. The term refers to the practice, favored by certain curators and critics, of compulsively quoting random phrases by philosophers such as Adorno, Baudrillard, Derrida, Deleuze, Nietszche and Benjamin. Adornamentation is characterized by stating a concept that bears no relationship to the topic that is being in discussion. It is often used to prevent any potential criticism of an essay, as the random mention of the quote requires the potential critic to go back and consult the original text—which generally is a very time-consuming and ultimately distracting task.

Aesthetics
Strategy.

Alternative Space
Exhibition space that shows the same kind of art as any art gallery, with the difference that those in charge do not know how to sell art.

Amnesia
Collective and voluntary project in which most art magazines, artists and contemporary curators participate, by pretending certain works, really the imitations of works made three or four decades ago are, indeed,

original. The benefits of amnesia include creating the impression that there is definitely something new under the sun, as well as the impression that the AW is progressing toward a new horizon.

Architecture
An esoteric term in the AW. When it is used, it conveys the impression of complexity in an art work. It is considered much more sophisticated to reference the history of architecture in a painting than the history of painting itself.

Art
An area of recycled human activity where bad architecture, ethnography, anthropology, and social and political theory find fertile grounds to develop and acquire new and exciting dimensions.

Art Education
An extremely arduous practice, in itself completely lacking in interest to the intellectual elite of the AW (curators and critics) but which is always included in exhibition proposals. It is supported by museum directors because it generates revenue from governments and foundations. Most museums receive tens of thousands of dollars for education programs, in exchange for purchasing a few boxes of crayons and offering workshops with volunteers. Recently, many artists and curators in the AW have claimed a stake in this lucrative area.

Artforum
Monthly publication considered as the official magazine of the AW club. Originally conceived to transmit content, it was deemed necessary to add 275 additional pages of advertising to it, allowing 25 pages for the interesting conversations between the editors and their friends.

Art History
Literary genre whose market is being dominated by five American universities, as well as the Courtauld Institute in Britain. Academics in those universities are known as novelists-in-residence. Originally, the art history genre took Anglo-Saxon and other European artists as main characters. This started changing in the '90s, thanks to collectors who

sponsored product-insertion campaigns in art historical surveys (also known as "epic novels").

Art School

Any institution that teaches nineteenth century art techniques, twentieth century art history, and asks students to pay tuitions at the rate of the upcoming century, with the assumption that art students will be able to navigate the present on their own.

Auction

Events where one finally abandons the pretense that art has an abstract value, and which exemplify the idea that the ultimate objective of owning art is to sell it. At auctions, the goal is to increase the sale price of the work above the price paid for it. When a work does not sell, the prices of the artist may collapse, in which case the artist himself may have to buy the piece in order to prevent his prices from dropping.

Avant-Garde

Art of antiquity, before the invention of art fairs.

Baroquism

Art criticism method consists of obscuring the meaning of something being said in order to add an esoteric layer to the work being analyzed. The philosophy of Baroquism applies especially in countries where political rhetoric has fused to such an extent with the life and culture of the society that it appears in all art-related writing. Baroquism works like quicksand: the more one tries to move around the text, the deeper the confusion. Like the art of magic, Baroquism meets the requirement of distracting the viewer with ideas that are so complex they are ultimately forgotten.

Baroquism uses the juxtaposition of opposites, with the objective of having each element cancel one another. Ideas usually follow the formula (A)+ (-A) = 0. The system can become much more complicated, as it is seen in the following phrase:

"The profound reasoning of his work constitutes a definitive affirmation of everyday living, in the same way in which his absolute negation of daily life is the final product of his intuitive austerity," in which we can see the following structural relationship:

$A \times B =$	$(C+D) \times$	E
profound reasoning	definitive affirmation	daily living
$(-C-D) \times$	$(E) =$	$(-A \times -B)$
absolute negation	daily life	intuitive austerity

As a result, by canceling affirmative and negative sentences, we arrive at a perfectly ambiguous and noncommittal commentary about the artist.

Beauty
This is a taboo subject in the AW, usually employed with negative connotations. Claiming to see beauty in something arouses suspicions, since the assessment of beauty tends to be regarded as from someone without selective taste. It can, however, have great impact when one evokes the word in as a metaphor, or in describing a work that is decisively repulsive.

Biennial
A marketing concept invented sometime in the nineteenth century, with the supposition that it would be interesting to invite the best artists in the world to the same place every two years to see their work. The proliferation of biennials has resulted in a deficit of ideas; today there are more biennials than rational subjects for a biennial. As a result, some biennial curators have started to choose irrational subjects, such as "the government of nothing" or "the tyranny of rebelliousness." Some critics warn that, may this trend continue, toward 2030 we will have run out of subjects for international biennials. Others argue that irrational subjects, like irrational numbers in mathematics, are infinite.

Buddhism
Spiritual practice embraced by some artists in the AW in order to show their regards for others, which usually holds true as long as the practitioner is given due credit and recognition for having adopted such a selfless practice.

Bullshit
Widely employed language strategy in the AW, with the function of taking the place of a lacking content. Bullshit is very effective when one wants to draw the attention of the public to an artwork that has no content whatsoever. Everyone in the AW should master the difficult art of Bullshit. Bullshit can be a highly effective mode of ice-breaking during openings and it is expected to be used at most important social occasions.

Catalogue
An object that accompanies the exhibition with the purpose of proving that the exhibition is important. The importance of the exhibition is directly proportional to the size of the catalogue. Catalogues usually have printed words in them, known as curatorial essays, signed by obscure authors. Often, these authors are also the only readers.

Conceptualism
Term that refers to the new academy. Conceptualism got established on the '60s as a explicit strategy. Today, no international artist who takes him or herself seriously can talk about his or her work without linking it somehow to the conceptual tradition. Whereas pure conceptualism is hard to sell, conceptualist layers in a work are as essential today in a work as chiaroscuro was in panting during the seventeenth century.

Conflict of Interest
Term that refers to the professional strategy of pushing personal agendas while pretending that one is pursuing exclusively artistic purposes. Once considered a sacrilege to art, the routinely application of the conflict of interest—and its great success—has finally obliterated the Kantian premise that the art experience needs to be essentially unselfish.

Connoisseur
A term defined by Ambroise Bierce as a person who knows everything about a given topic, while ignoring everything about any other topic. In the AW, *connoisseurs* narrow their area of knowledge even more, focusing only on artworks that are marketable, or specialties that lead to tenure-track positions.

Compromise
Unspoken transaction between AW professionals through which one obtains more or less what he or she seeks by accepting small losses on their side, whether they be credibility, career, or money.

Craft
Outmoded genre in art that ruled the aesthetic of a whole era, from the Middle Ages until the nineteenth century, when artists had manual abilities that would distinguish them from those who did not have them. When the craft dictatorship fell to the Avant-Garde, artists who had stronger verbal abilities designed the program for contemporary art. Despite this historic triumph, every now and then there is a vague nostalgia for that previous dictatorial time.

Curiosity
A feature of art-making now extinct in the AW, having been determined useless. When flourishes spontaneously in the work of a young artist, it will soon be extinguished by demands of mass production.

Derivation (or, Made in Taiwan)
A stabilizing process in the AW that consists of imitating existing products at a lower quality in order to satisfy mass demand. Derivation yields a line of works whose basic features, both formally and conceptually, have been already firmly established by another artist. Although derivative art rarely receives favorable critical acceptance, it keeps the AW well provided with alternative purchase choices for collectors who cannot afford to obtain the truly original works.

Determinism
Theory that, despite the colossal failure of multiculturalism, affirms that geographic origin, gender, skin color, religion, sexual orientation or nationality in an artist are necessarily his or her favorite subjects, as well as his or her specialty, particularly when the artist in question is not white, European, male, and heterosexual. Since there is a wide market for determinist art, entire nations, along with the collaboration of their artists, make special efforts to produce it. As a result, determinism is a self-fulfilling prophecy, generating a demand that is quickly satisfied.

Determinist art is not capable of sincerity, but as it borders on illustration, this fact is usually not an obstacle.

Dia

Protestant sect that has promoted the canonization of twenty or so artists. In the highly secular world of the AW, where religion is often looked down upon, Dia has helped to change that perception. Most recently, the congregation created a museum in Beacon, offering permanent sanctuary to these artists on the track to sainthood. As a result, Dia Beacon has become a common pilgrimage site for contemporary art enthusiasts.

Documentation

In theory, this is a method to prove that an artwork existed or exists. In practical terms, photographic documentation is a useful tool to make a saleable record of a non-material work (performance, site-specific installation, etc.). The invention of Photoshop has additionally helped in generating documentation of works that never existed in the real world.

Dwarfs on Shoulders of Giants (or DSG)

This phrase refers to mediocre artists who have achieved recognition by establishing close friendships or connections with more famous and older artists. DSG can be detected in artists who heavily refer to these artists in their work or who derive symbolic capital by becoming caretakers of remarkable artists at the end of their careers and who are elderly and slightly senile.

Emerging Artist

Artists (and galleries) are described as "emerging" (also known as "C-level" artists) when they have not yet received international recognition or when their careers are beginning. Still, since the term is fairly vague, many artists choose to remain emerging for life, especially when their careers have not particularly taken off.

Gesamtkunstwerk

Any project by Matthew Barney, or any art project with a budget of 5 million dollars or more.

High Modernism
Branch of contemporary art that references the works related to Modernism but with excessive pretensions.

Impostor
Negative manner of referring to an artist (and in some cases, a curator) who makes the effort to create work not in response to his own interests but rather in response to the interests of the market. In general, those who are labeled as "impostors" have an acute commercial sense, and are capable of quickly recognizing demand and product availability, and as in any business, generating an effective and marketable product.

Immorality
An aesthetic recourse of great impact that recently has proved very pleasing in the AW. Immoral works are often considered witty and entertaining and help AW members to emphasize their openness—with the exception of works that, as it has been pointed out in this manual, may be offensive to collectors.

Immortality
Insurance policy in the AW that curators give to artists and is paid for by collectors. In exchange, the collectors become immortalized by museums when galleries are named after them.

Institutional Critique
Conceptual choreography used by some artists in order to acquire fame by demonizing the museum institution and contemporary art's academic infrastructure. These artists are usually very popular in museums and universities, which invite them to their panels, exhibitions and events in order to prove that they are open to criticism.

Interdisciplinary
Use of other areas of human knowledge by artists in order to compensate for their lack of resources or visual vocabulary.

Kosher

New York term referring to situations where political correctness is adequately being employed. In the AW, the term is applied to diverse situations. For example, when a museum invites an outside curator to give a lecture about a subject that is the expertise of the house curator, it is considered *unkosher*. Inviting a woman or an artist of color to a predominantly white male exhibition is considered *kosher*.

Land Art

Art genre, invented by Robert Smithson, Walter de Maria and Michael Heizer in the sixties in order to question the museum as a sacred space. Today, the works of these artists have become sacred and can be seen at your nearest museum.

Localism

Schizophrenic condition often suffered by artists living on the periphery, who on the one hand reject their local artistic environment in order to embrace their internationalist environment, while at the same time affirm their individuality by emphasizing their connection with their local culture.

Minimalism

Art form created by the Brazilian neo-concretists and adopted by a group of American artists who were afraid of sharing their feelings with the public.

MoMA

The AW's most influential banking institution. MoMA is the holder of works of very high value assigned by art history (the academic-literary world) and the market. The board of trustees ensures that the works of the artists they decide to collect remain highly valued.

Multiculturalism

Movement invented by mediocre artists of color, who argued that the poor quality of their works was in fact a mistaken interpretation of their secret cultural symbolism, which is profoundly misunderstood by the white male AW.

Museum
In developed countries, it is a banking warehouse that organizes fun events for its local club. In countries where government runs the arts, museums are empty spaces that are built only for the day of the opening with the president in attendance, and with the objective of holding all the efforts of the syndicated workers who do not wish to work and to provide directorships for the politician's wives.

Namedropping
The term refers to the casually use of the personal names of famous AW figures in the course of a conversation. Namedropping is a strategic action employed by those who seek to establish their social and professional status during a given interaction. The first name of the person is used in order to show familiarity ("Marina," "Jeff," "Matthew," etc.), and also as an elitist code that one could identify only if one also belongs to the elite.

New Media
Term promoted in the 1990s as part of an effort to create a new artistic genre based on programming and software. The rise of the Internet gave way to this new genre, and toward 1999 every other artist was a new media artist. But due to the boredom caused by not being able to see (or buy) interesting physical objects, the contemporary fatigue caused by scrutinizing a monitor, and the anxiety of new media artists not being treated as real artists in museums, the artists started abandoning their new media definition and lobbied to be accepted again as simple "artists."

Opportunism
The latest and most successful "ism" in art. It can acquire many forms, but its basic aesthetic position is that contemporary art must adopt the form of the opportunity presented at any given moment. For instance, an artist who has never done video should immediately "become" a video artist if an exhibition opportunity for that medium comes his or her way. The same applies to themes: when a curator mentions a topic of his or her interest, the artist should pretend to show extreme surprise and then say that he or she incidentally is working on a series of pieces on that precise subject. The opportunist artist is particularly compat-

ible with the artistic curator, who often concocts ideas *a priori* and then seeks out artists to illustrate them.

Ornamental
The term is often used to describe any motif or component in a work that has no other function than simply "being there," supposedly improving the aesthetic experience as a flavorful component, but without taking center stage. Ornamentalism has had its very own development over the course of the twentieth century. Although in earlier times Ornamentalism consisted of making marginal decorative forms of classical attributes, today's artists have managed to ornamentalize most components of conceptual art. Political content in a work can be merely ornamental in the same way in which allegorical paintings ornamentalized ideas during the eighteenth century.

Painting
Art medium that is systematically declared dead, so that prices can go up every time there is a resurrection.

Performance Art
Term coined by a group of utopians to refer to a series of attitudes and aesthetic positions that questioned, amongst other things, the commercialization of art and the border between art and life. Later on, some thought it convenient to turn the term into an art genre, its documentation into saleable items, and its history as useful to fund academic research positions. The performance art specialists who work in academia often are happy to adopt the position of referee, adjudicating endorsements about what is or is not acceptable as a performance art piece.

Photoshop
The greatest artistic invention of the twentieth century.

Plagiarism
A form of indirect homage to an original artist, pretending that the original artist does not exist. The practitioners of plagiarism propose, as part of their work, a utopian world where those from whom they derive their ideas will always remain unknown to the audience.

Poetic Criticism
Literary genre created by uninspired poets who use artworks in order to write literary fantasies that they themselves define as "art criticism." The artists from whom these writers find inspiration are generally of a pre-conceptual order, because in order to execute poetic criticism one has to depart from the premise that the artist only feels without thinking.

Politically Correct
Art philosophy that argues it is better to die of boredom than risk hurting anybody's feelings.

Problematize
In art critical terminology, to "problematize" means to turn any topic into a fertile philosophical ground to make works for market consumption.

Public Art
Cultural tradition consisting of commissioning artworks that would take as much space as possible in an urban environment, so that they can be restored and preserved by future generations.

Referentiality
Artistic strategy that consists of creating works that make direct reference to established artists or artworks, supposedly as an homage, but actually with the secret hopes that the simple act of choosing such reference will raise the value of the referential work.

Relational Aesthetics
Philosophical trend initiated by French curator Nicolás Bourriaud, and which justified the tendency of artists and curators to travel to exotic locations and use local communities as the source of their work.

RSVP
Letters by which AW members assess the level of their status. Professional influence is directly proportional to the amount of RSVP events to which one is invited. As a result, and even when an event is not that special, institutions often seek to organize as many RSVP events as possible

with the hopes of make their members feel included in a certain degree of exclusivity.

Situationism
Intellectual movement of the 1960s that attempted to change society, and which now has been adopted as a strategy to create marketing campaigns.

Slide
Form of photographic documentation that was invented more than half a century ago and which is extinct in the real world. It is still the official documentation format of the AW.

Speculation
Common strategy in the AW describing the influence of rising and falling popularity of a certain work and artist while one reaps benefits during the process. Speculation is, like insider trading, the easiest way to generate economic revenue, with the difference that the AW is not closely watched nor legally penalized for these actions. Speculation works best when it is controlled by a curator who can influence the purchase of a work while at the same time controlling the selection of an artist. The process can be as follows:

1. A curator from an international museum or biennial (who by including the work of an artists guarantees his or her growth in value) offers the inclusion of this artist in the show as long as the curator receives (or his institution, or his clients) one or several works by this artist at the pre-exhibition price.
2. A museum curator creates a secret alliance with a gallery that will offer him a percentage of the sales of work by an artist included in a museum exhibition. Both the gallery and the artist benefit by the museum endorsement, and all are benefited financially.
3. A collector influences a museum to exhibit the works of one of the artists in his collection—a process which often helps to increment the value of the works in the collector's possession.

Success
Social status that is rarely attained when one looks for it, and which sometimes is obtained by mistake. Repeating the same mistakes can often lead to even more success. In very rare circumstances, a good artist can also be a successful one.

Symposia
Social event often attended by those members of the AW that are involved in its discursive component. Symposia usually do not include enough time to have discussions, given that 89% of the time is devoted to introductions and presentations. In general, it is estimated that the public can only comprehend only 9% of a read presentation and the 15% of a spoken one. This is due to a lack of adaptation of a theoretical text to the stage presentation, and the lack of theatrical experience of most critics, artists and historians who participate in symposia. Symposia are the basis of dialogue and communication in the AW.

Symposia about Biennials
Symposia that are organized by international biennials where curators are invited to say that the biennial model has been exhausted, and that there is no other model but to continue being invited to symposia in order to speak about the exhausted model of the international biennial.

Vanity Gallery
Adult fantasy service for artists who are dying to exhibit in New York. The personnel from these galleries are trained to attract clueless artists who wander around spaces in SoHo (since they think that the "art scene" is still located there) and quickly offer them a solo exhibition. Most aspiring artists will sign the exhibition agreement without realizing that it involves renting the gallery space for thousands of dollars.

Zeitgeist
German word that translates to the "spirit of the times." In the AW, it is understood as those trends that are "in the air." Zeitgeist is decided upon by a small group of collectors who meet on a regular basis. Such leadership has provided a great relief to artists, curators, and critics, who no longer have to deal with the ambiguities of uncertain times.

ABOUT THE AUTHOR

Pablo Helguera is a visual artist. Some of his past art projects, which have come close to breaking every etiquette rule, have included making a phonographic archive of dying languages, creating scripted symposia performed by actors (unbeknownst to the audience), building a memory theater, and founding a research institute exploring the global impact of Latin American soap operas. Most recently, he drove from Anchorage to Tierra del Fuego with a collapsible schoolhouse, organizing discussions and civic ceremonies (The School of Panamerican Unrest). He lives in Brooklyn.

www.ingramcontent.com/pod-product-compliance
Lightning Source LLC
LaVergne TN
LVHW091006080826
845145LV00003B/1145

* 9 7 8 0 9 7 9 0 7 6 6 0 2 *